Portraits of S

The Manitoulin School of Art Comes of Age

Text and Photography by Margo Little

Cover Art By
James Mishibinijima

Feel The Spirit,
Margo Little

The author gratefully acknowledges the support of the Ontario Arts Council Writers' Works in Progress Program.

ONTARIO ARTS COUNCIL
CONSEIL DES ARTS DE L'ONTARIO

Layout by Mandy Pickard, Kenjgewin Teg Educational Institute.

A special thank you to HighGrader Magazine.

HIGH GRADER
M·A·G·A·Z·I·N·E
A VOICE FROM THE NORTHLAND
Canadian Publication Mail Contract No. 0622796

Library and Archives Canada Cataloguing in Publication

Little, Margo, 1947-
Portraits of Spirit Island : the Manitoulin School of Art comes of age / text and photography by Margo Little ; cover art by James Mishibinijima.

Includes bibliographical reference
ISBN 978-0-9685047-2-7

1. Indian artists--Ontario--Manitoulin Island--Biography. 2. Artists--Ontario--Manitoulin Island--Biography. 3. Art, Canadian--Ontario--Manitoulin Island. 4. Manitoulin Island (Ont.)--Biography. I. Title.

N6549.5.A54L58 2009 704.03'9707131350922 C2009-902734-8

• • • •

Author's Prologue

In the spring of 2007 I started publishing a series of articles on the Manitou arts in Highgrader Magazine based in Timmins, Ontario. My intention was to showcase some of the Manitoulin artists who are often renowned internationally, but somewhat neglected in their own back yard. For several months, I visited artists in their studios and galleries to document their life stories and struggles for recognition in the fickle world of Canadian fine art.

Then in the fall of the same year I had the opportunity to present a paper at "Witness: A Symposium on the Woodland School," organized by curator/artist Bonnie Devine at Laurentian University in Sudbury. The event was held in conjunction with Daphne Odjig's retrospective exhibition at the Art Gallery of Sudbury. In tandem with Alan Corbiere, director of the Ojibwe Cultural Foundation (OCF), I presented a lecture and slide show introducing a national audience to some of the Manitoulin artists who produce their works in relative seclusion on this special island.

I felt compelled to see these stories told for a number of reasons. For twenty years I had been attending events at the Ojibwe Cultural Foundation and publishing articles on the work to preserve Anishinaabe language, customs and history. I always felt irresistibly drawn to the OCF and connected to the local landscape and people because my ancestor Louis Corbiere was a store keeper in West Bay in 1876. And my great-grandparents, Henry (1877-1959) and Katherine Corbiere (1877-1957), had operated a tea-room on the land where the current OCF stands. My mother, a member of M'Chigeeng First Nation, had always told me stories about visiting her grandparents at their business on that site (circa 1929.)

Although I believed the stories of the artists were clamouring to be expressed, I did feel some misgivings and doubt as I conducted the interviews. Was I being too intrusive? Was it appropriate for me to approach these artists and ask them to share their sources of inspiration? Should I be the one relating these tales and revealing the wellspring of their creativity?

But as I was welcomed into their homes and workplaces, my self-trust and sense of purpose returned. Soon I was delving into the past at the OCF library and combing through the archives, old exhibition catalogues, magazine articles and minutes of board meetings trying to get an overall picture of the origins of the organization and the artists it served.

It was during this time that I received a nighttime visitation encouraging me to carry on. On October 3, 2007, I dreamed I was at the OCF rehearsing the slide show and talk I had prepared for the symposium. As I projected the photographs of the artists and their paintings on to the screen, a ghostly figure in a white robe rose up beside each image. The phantom wasn't sure of my intentions at first. She was watching, observing, bearing witness. At first I thought she might rebuke me. But then, to my great joy, she gave me her blessing. “Yes, this is a good thing,” she said. “Yes, you must preserve the history.”

When her presence faded, I was left with the comforting feeling that she would still be watching me closely, but she was pleased. I sensed she was supportive of the work I was doing. With her approval, it would be my mission to help the forgotten ones tell their stories.

With the dream as my guide, I set forth to demonstrate that the island arts still flourish and the Manitoulin School of Art has indeed come of age.

Dedication

This book is dedicated to the memory of Thomas Elvin Peltier "Jomin" (February 2, 1936 to April 5, 2009).

Thomas passed away on April 5, 2009, in Wikwemikong at the age of 73 years. He is remembered as a man of vision who worked for many years to promote and preserve First Nations art and heritage. One of his most memorable projects was the Indian Pavilion established at Expo 67 in Montreal where Aboriginal artists received international exposure. Another lasting legacy was the Manitou Arts Project, which assembled young Native artists from many diverse communities for summer art camps at Schreiber Island. Thomas was actively involved in politics, working under former Prime Ministers Pierre Elliot Trudeau and Jean Chretien. He was also a very fine writer, penning the best-selling book *Bearwalk,* as well as the novel-in-progress, *Dakota Rose.*

Many of the artists he encouraged and supported over the past forty years have established careers in North America and overseas.

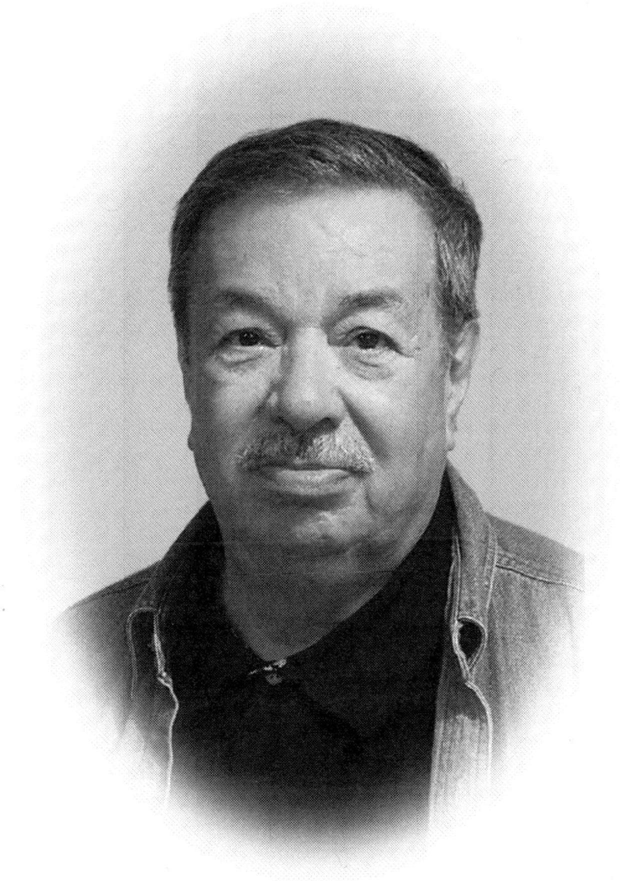

Preface

Manitoulin Island, the jewel of Georgian Bay, stretches along the North shore of Lake Huron. With a land mass covering 2,775 kilometres, the island is 160 kms long and from three to 65 kms wide. Manitoulin takes its name from the Algonkian word Manitoulain signifying "Den of the Manitou." Despite its small size, Spirit Island has always been a source of power and energy. Although it has not always been a hospitable environment, it has spawned a remarkable group of dynamic artists.

The artists of the Manitoulin School of Art have persisted and endured despite pressures from outside forces to mould them into a style more acceptable to the Canadian art establishment. Many of these unique artists have been severely tested by life circumstances and prevailing mainstream perceptions, yet they have emerged from trying times with their individuality and integrity intact.

Author and consultant Tom Peltier, of Wikwemikong Unceded Reserve, has witnessed the emergence of many young artists over the past four decades. In the early 60s, he had been present at Norval Morrisseau's first ground-breaking exhibition. And he returned home convinced that there were talented individuals in his community and in other First Nations who were producing unique canvases as well. For example, he noticed young people such as Francis Kagige, patiently working away in an attic and creating imagery similar to Morrisseau. In those days, Daphne Odjig often came home to Wikwemikong and she too was painting in a distinctive way.

Mr. Peltier believed that Aboriginal artists were hampered by government policies and by long-standing stereotypes. Later, he would use his influence to ensure that First Nations artists had a chance to be represented at Canada's Expo 67, in Montreal.

"We got in there and got a piece of property and started to build a pavilion," he recalled. "We brought in a whole bunch of people to help us design the building. We were the last ones to get started and the first ones to finish."

Eventually, the artists took the project out of the hands of the Indian Affairs Department and formed their own corporation to get the pavilion finished. The international tourists who flooded the Expo grounds were greeted with eight murals completed by Aboriginal artists.

Although there were many more obstacles to overcome, stereotypes were slowly eroding, in his view.

"A year and a half later Hollywood brought out the movie, *A Man Called Horse* and the year after that they released *Little Big Man*," he noted.

The Expo experience would have a lasting impact on Tom as well as associates such as Duke Redbird and Alex Janvier. As artists they had first hand experience with the roadblocks facing Native youth and they were motivated to make some positive changes. Coincidentally, the Ontario Institute for Studies in Education (OISE) was conducting a study in Wikwemikong at the time, to ascertain why so many students were dropping out of school. Mr. Peltier wasn't convinced that another survey would net any improvements. Instead, he and a collective of artists resolved to try another way to reach Native students.

"I was a high school drop-out myself, so I decided to take on OISE and try something different with an alternative project," he quipped.

The Manitou Arts Foundation was established in 1966 and by 1971, funding was in place. The now legendary Schreiber Island project would turn out to be the incubator and catalyst for many youngsters in need of a boost to their self-esteem and sense of direction.

"We scouted out Schreiber Island and we gathered twenty five to thirty artists such as Daphne Odjig, Duke Redbird and Carl Ray. We had a whole host of fairly good people," he said. "We went and did our little project and it turned out very well. Of course, at the beginning we didn't know what we were getting into."

He speculates that the experiment worked precisely because it was not an OISE study or an academic exercise. They welcomed young people from throughout the north in their first year and put them in an environment where they could grow in confidence and skill.

"At Schreiber, there were no rules; it was all hands on," he said. "We didn't want to have an assembly line atmosphere or a clock on the wall. Instead, we gave them tents and we let them sleep until noon. We gave them privacy and that made all the difference in the world."

The instructors developed close relationships with the novice artists offering them tutoring in drama, painting, music and photography. Role models such as Daphne Odjig and others would encourage the youth to explore the rocks, plants and wildlife in the idyllic setting. It was not uncommon for students to stay up late and paint well into the night.

Film-making also helped many a shy teenager come out of his or her shell and take advantage of the creative outlets and resources provided.

"We filmed them from the moment they got off the bus and then we let the kids make a film too. There was no script; we just let them follow a process and let them find out how their minds worked. It's a different approach to education, a different way of knowledge. There are lots of different ways of doing the same thing," he reiterated.

The program ran from 1971 to 1973. Over the years Tom Peltier remained a strong advocate for arts in the school curriculum. He continued to believe that art and music can inspire children to not only stay in school, but to flourish.

By all accounts, the arts had many champions during the 1970s and seeds were sown for a rich harvest to come.

In 1973, the Ojibwe Cultural Foundation (OCF) was established in West Bay (now known as M'Chigeeng.) It was dedicated to the preservation of the rich heritage of the

Ojibwe, Pottawatomi and Odawa people. The founders wanted to have a museum quality building to house the priceless art collections and to make the art readily accessible to the communities. Mary Lou Fox, a former Manitoulin Secondary School teacher and Department of Indian Affairs consultant, served as the first executive director.

Although she often stressed that "Indian people have no word for art," she worked tirelessly to demonstrate that Native art is alive, distinctive and real. In her view, "The arts and crafts of the Indian people are founded on a spiritual culture as enduring as the earth. Art is a part of life, like hunting, like fishing, like growing food, like having a family," she emphasized. "This is art in its broadest sense - an object of daily usefulness, to be admired and appreciated, nurturing the needs of both body and soul, thereby giving meaning to everything."

As she and her supporters pursued their dream, they had to be content with modest facilities at first. A converted general store with the gas pumps removed was used for their home base. Later, a trailer portable would be added to house the growing collection. When they were first incorporated in 1974, the First Nations at West Bay, Sheshegwaning, Sucker Creek, Sheguiandah, Wikwemikong, Birch Island and Sagamok all endorsed the charter. Later, in 1976, all of the bands between Sudbury and North Bay, including those along the route to Parry Sound, were included.

The mandate to promote Indian artists locally, regionally, nationally and internationally was taken very seriously. Artists were able to access art supplies through the OCF. They were also taught basic skills such as how to stretch canvas and how to make frames. Manitoulin artists received assistance in exhibiting their art at the OCF, in Sudbury and overseas in Italy and Switzerland.

Of all their initiatives, the OCF summer camps that ran 1974-1977, were some of the most memorable. At settings such as Dreamer's Rock and Rainbow Lodge on Birch Island, youngsters basked in the influence of older artists for two weeks at a time. Many developed their own styles by the end of the interactive sessions.

With many budding young artists emerging from the art camps, it became imperative to keep providing resources and support for their careers. Again the Ojibwe Cultural Foundation demonstrated ambitious goals. In 1978, the OCF attempted to bring artists from across the country to Manitoulin Island to share their experiences, views, insights and resources. The First National Native Artists' Conference was launched October 23-25. Funded by Indian and Northern Affairs Canada and the Secretary of State, it aimed to create a congregation of all the luminaries in the Native art scene in Canada. In an article published in The Native Perspective magazine (Vol. 3, #2, 1978), it was suggested that the conference failed to meet its lofty objectives since it drew only 35 participants. However, it was undoubtedly a landmark event in that it succeeded in attracting established artists such as Daphne Odjig, Bill Reid and Alex Janvier. It did give some young artists a chance to rub shoulders with influential mentors and to express their thoughts on culture and art.

In the 1980s, Mary Lou Fox continued her mission to revive and preserve Aboriginal arts, not just locally but provincially as well. In June 1981, for instance, she helped co-ordinate K'wech-Ku-da-d'win, the first provincial Native craft conference at Erindale College in Mississauga, Ontario. According to the report issued after the event, it was the first time Native people had gathered on a provincial level to discuss their concerns about the marketing and the quality control of Aboriginal artworks. Leading up to the southern Ontario conference, a series of smaller craft consultations had been held in Sudbury, Brantford, Quetico, Timmins and Cornwall Island. At group discussions, artists had an opportunity to share perspectives on everything from pricing of handmade items to symbolism in the artworks. Manitoulin crafts such as quilts, beadwork, moccasins, jewellery, quill baskets and split ash baskets were sold at the June 3-6 gathering.

Also participating in the K'wech-ku-da-d'win workshops was Gerald McMaster, curator of Contemporary Indian Art at the National Museum of Man in Ottawa. He too was concerned about the loss of many traditional arts and the advent of mass production machinery that threatened to destroy quality and authenticity. In a speech delivered to the 1981 conference, he stressed the need to preserve technical and visual excellence despite the destructive influences of the reserve and residential school systems. He noted that many Native artists had successfully looked to the past for inspiration and combined traditional indigenous designs with present day materials and techniques. He observed that artists who interpreted the past and filtered it through modern realities were producing creative, original and contemporary art. He also urged his listeners to use the work of other artists as a springboard for their own knowledge and skill development.

By the 1990s, the OCF had long since outgrown its cramped quarters in the former general store in M'Chigeeng. It would take patience and persistence to acquire a new facility.

In 1996, Ms. Fox announced her retirement after twenty five years at the helm. In her parting remarks during a gathering at Birch Island, she expressed satisfaction that the OCF had been able to host the first national gathering of Native artists in 1978 and the first national gathering of Aboriginal Elders in 1993. "Manitoulin is a very special place, but we also have the human resources here," she told the Manitoulin Expositor on December 11, 1996. "I think that it is significant that we were asked to host these two major national gatherings."

Although retired, Ms. Fox carried on with fund raising efforts for the project dear to her heart. On August 6, 1997, the board kicked off a capital building campaign to construct a new home for the valuable collection of art and artifacts. The Ontario Historical Society Bulletin reported in their September/October issue that the OCF had already raised a substantial portion of the $2.7 million needed, but needed to access an additional $750,000. Supporters included the Ontario Ministry of Culture and Recreation, Northern Ontario Heritage Fund, FedNor, Heritage Canada and the Department of Indian Affairs.

People came from near and far to pay tribute to Ms. Fox during an emotional evening at the OCF October 4, 1997. At that time an award was founded in her name and the Mary Lou Fox Resource Centre and Library was unveiled. "The Mary Lou Fox Founder's Award," is given annually to the person who has made a notable contribution to the language, arts and culture of the Ojibway, Odawa and Potowatami peoples. During the ceremony, Chief Diane Abotossaway of Aundeck Omni Kaning, described Ms. Fox as "a priceless jewel" to the Anishinabek Nation.

Manitoulin lost one of its strongest supporters of heritage, culture and the arts when Mary Lou Fox passed away April 26, 1998. Known as Ode-min Kwe (Heart Berry Woman), she had devoted her life to preserving the stories, songs, language and arts of the Anishinaabe people. In her lifetime she was honoured with the "Order of Ontario" and recognized for her outstanding service to history and heritage preservation in Ontario. She also received honourary doctoral degrees from Laurentian University and Brock University.

Although the OCF has faced financial hurdles since the New Millenium, it has survived the economic hardships and reaffirmed the convictions of the founders. In 2004, over 40 artists attended a symposium and gala marking the tenth anniversary of the Manitoulin Art Tour. And in 2007 and 2008, the summer art camps that were so well-received in the mid-70s, were revived for a whole new generation of First Nations youth to enjoy. They had a chance to interact with the some of the now mature artists who had found their calling decades ago at Schreiber Island.

For researcher Alan Corbiere, the Manitoulin School of Art has always been a source of endless fascination. In his capacity as OCF executive director (2007-2009), the young historian had made it a priority to showcase Manitoulin artists, both established and emerging, at the M'Chigeeng centre. In the process, he delved into the archives and created an overview of the origins of Anishinaabe art.

Although the Manitoulin School of Art is often viewed as synonymous with the Woodland School, Mr. Corbiere contends that it "may not necessarily be so." In his view, Manitoulin artists cannot be pigeon-holed in that manner. Although many may have started out using Woodland techniques, most have branched off into highly individual personal styles.

"The work in the Manitoulin School of Art is more varied than people might assume," he said. "Culture is not static, as you know, and neither is art. Anishinaabe art is not all tomtoms and teepees as some might think. On the contrary, our culture has great depth and great breadth. In the past these shows were held in museums because that was the prevailing sentiment in the 70s and 80s. But we hope to see more of our diverse artists in the National Gallery one day."

• • • •

Table of Contents

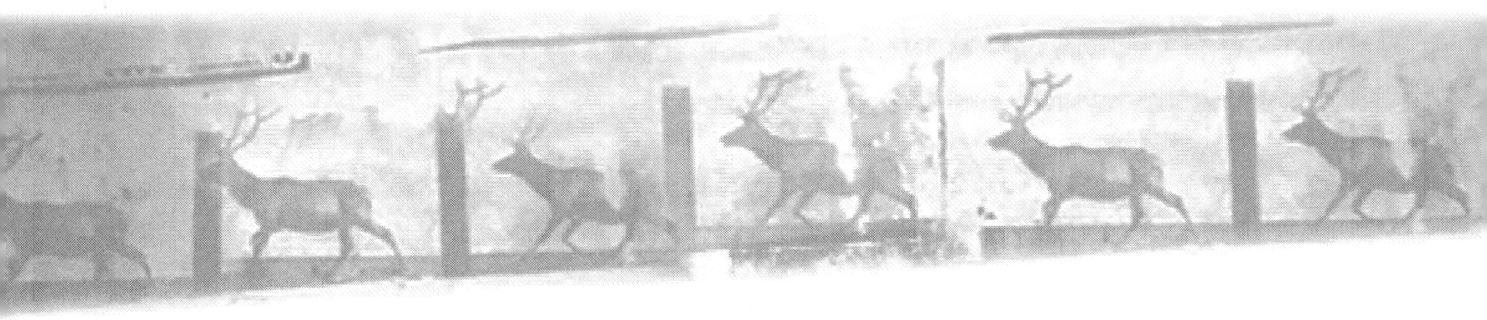

CARL, ANN AND ANONG BEAM: IT'S ALL RELATIVE

CARL BEAM (1943 - 2005): Burying the Ruler

CHAPTER 1

Some works of art dare the viewer to react or to pause and reflect. M'Chigeeng First Nation artist Carl Beam created the kind of open-ended and ambiguous pieces that compelled people to stop and think. His images were often unsettling because they elicited both emotional and intellectual responses. He had mastered the knack of appealing to the subconscious through cleverly arranged symbols and allusions. An encounter with a Carl Beam exhibit was an occasion for self-analysis and reassessment of personal value systems. Many people have been jolted out of their comfort zones by his subversive works.

In many ways his artwork involved a process of thinking out loud and examining life from different angles. He spent time musing on the significance of historical events, modern day crises and future possibilities. One can imagine him thumbing through periodicals, watching television, reading academic texts, looking at old photo albums, daydreaming, remembering and conjecturing. As he circled back in time, he collected images of places and objects that spoke to him and brought them forward to rest beside images of current technology and human progress.

In his personal quest for meaning, he was not afraid to examine human foibles in depth. But as he explored and experimented there was no preaching or dictating. That was not his way. Instead he posed thorny questions and set up brain teasers for the bystander to ponder. It was as if he was yearning for understanding himself and you were invited along on the journey. You were welcome to join him, but you shouldn't expect the trek to be easy; above all, you shouldn't expect to be spoon fed. Shaking off outmoded perceptions and re-ordering your priorities takes courage. In the end, you may have to accept that there are no pat answers or simple solutions, just more challenging questions.

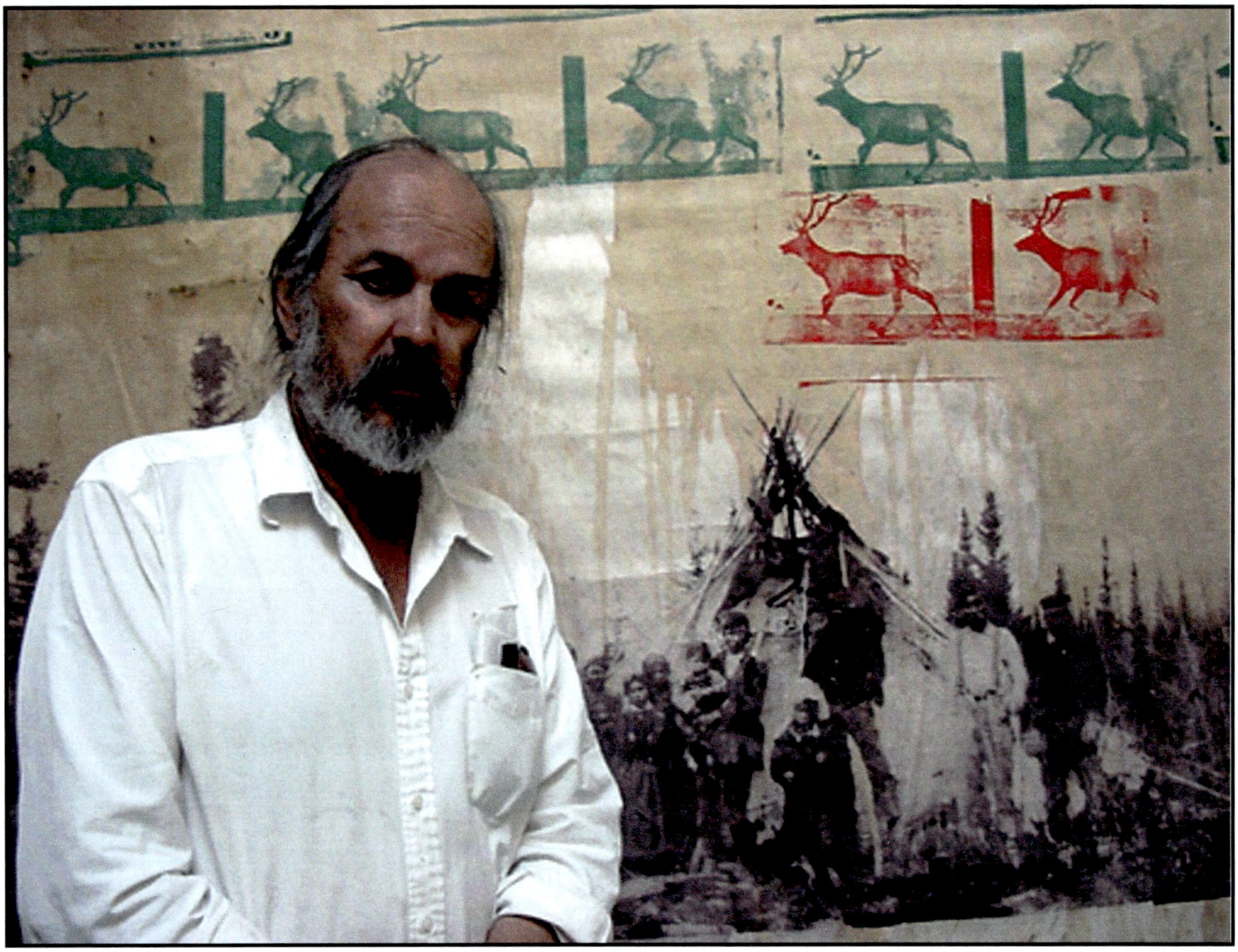

Carl Beam was born on Manitoulin Island. His mother was Ojibway and his father non-Native. His formative years were spent in a church-run boarding school, an experience that no doubt shaped many of his adult opinions and world view. Like other First Nations children from Manitoulin and the North Shore, he was transported to an institution located on a thousand acres at the mouth of the Spanish River. When it opened in 1913 it was known as St. Peter's school for boys; later it was renamed Garnier Residential School in honour of Charles Garnier, a Jesuit martyr killed by Huron warriors in early colonial days. Under the iron hand of their Catholic masters, the boys were housed in dormitories, forbidden to speak their language and deprived of contact with their parents. The government sanctioned this misguided assimilation campaign until Garnier was closed down in 1958. It stood for decades as a sinister reminder of the abuses perpetrated within its walls. Although it was boarded up in 1996 and finally demolished in 2004, untold damage was done. Students like Carl carried the imprint left by the Black Robes into their adult lives.

There would be many years of travelling and soul-searching before he heeded the call to become a full time artist. John K. Grande, author of Carl Beam: Dissolving Time, reports that Carl laboured at a variety of jobs including a stint in Toronto subway tunnel construction. He also worked as a millwright's assistant in Wawa and as a logger and sawmill hand in British Columbia.

In time he took up studies at the Kootenay School of Art (1971) and was inspired to earn a Bachelor of Fine Arts from the University of Victoria (1974). In addition, he conducted post-graduate studies at the University of Alberta (1975-76). He left the program after a disagreement over the direction of his thesis on Native art.

Surrounded by practitioners of the Woodland School, he chafed under the perceived limitations of medicine painting and set out to find his own individual style. He began to articulate his unique vision with a variety of media, including watercolour, etching, photo transfer, drawing, installation and pottery. He experimented with negatives or transparencies projected on to prepared surfaces in a darkroom. Cloudy images from the past would be mixed in with up-to-date current events. Highly technical references would mingle with the mundane. Sometimes he slathered paint over the disparate images to unify the theme. Intricate multi-imaged works combining archival photos, historical and scientific texts and stencilled or hand-written messages became the hallmark of his style.

Over the years his provocative and innovative works have been exhibited in North America and overseas. He participated in a show called "In the Shadow of the Sun" in Dortmund, Germany in 1989. That same year he joined the "Beyond History" exhibit at the Vancouver Art Gallery. 1992 was a banner year with the "Indigena" show at the Canadian Museum of Civilization in Hull, Quebec, as well as the "Land, Spirit and Power" exhibit at the National Gallery of Canada, Ottawa. In 1993, he was invited to the Newton Art Centre, Newtonville, Massachusetts for the "Fragile Power: Explorations of Memory" event. An international symposium took him to Santa Fe, New Mexico in 1993 as well. There he spoke on the concept behind *Burying the Ruler*. The Brandts Klaederfabrik gallery in Odense, Denmark hosted his *Indian Time* works in 1995 and he was part of the "Transitions" show held at the Canadian Cultural Centre in Paris (1997).

Of all his landmark exhibitions, *The Columbus Boat* caused a stir in Canada, the US and Italy. It was mounted at The Power Plant in Toronto in June 1992, at the Weil Gallery in Corpus Christie, Texas, and at Italian galleries in Milan, Bologna, Genoa and La Spezia.

His creations have been collected by such institutions as the National Gallery of Canada, the Museum of Civilization, the Art Gallery of Ontario, the McMicheal Collection of Canadian Art, the Vancouver Art Gallery and the Calgary Nickel Arts Museum.

History was made in 1986, when his large mixed media piece entitled *The North American Iceberg* was acquired by the National Gallery of Canada. It was the first time that the Ottawa institution had purchased a work by an Aboriginal artist as contemporary fine art and not as ethnographic art. The work was completed with acrylic paint and serigraphs on Plexiglas and included coverage of Anwar al-Sadat's assassination, a rocket lifting off, an encyclopaedia entry, a photo of Geronimo as well as an eagle, hand prints and archival photos of Native people.

Carl had produced the work in response to an Art Gallery of Ontario (AGO) exhibition featuring contemporary European artists. The AGO show had been preoccupied with the notion that current European trends were being disregarded in North American art. For Carl, the advent of the so-called European Iceberg was the perfect opportunity for him to reiterate some long held beliefs. During his student days he had spoken out about the neglect of Aboriginal history, culture and art. No one was listening then, but after his powerful rebuttal in *The North American Iceberg*, the Canadian art establishment had no choice but to pay attention. Collecting practices were starting to change nationally.

By the year 2000, he had been inducted into the Royal Canadian Academy of Arts.

A career built on resistance to stereotypes eventually battered down some doors and shattered some deeply ingrained attitudes. Carl's inventive and avant garde contributions were eventually recognized. On March 16, 2005, Carl was awarded the Governor General's Award for visual and media arts in recognition of a lifetime of artistic achievement. He accepted the $15,000 prize for his outstanding body of work from then Governor General Adrienne Clarkson.

Although he passed away July 30, 2005, his work continues to generate interest among art historians and critics across Canada and internationally. Academics never tire of analysing, categorizing, pigeon-holing and dissecting the sometimes esoteric, sometimes ironic messages in his work. No doubt Carl Beam's artistic statements will provide fodder for the art establishment for decades to come.

However, Manitoulin residents remember a more down to earth and accessible Carl Beam. For instance, he was one of the prime movers behind the "Festival of Thanksgiving," held August 6-11, 1984. Six Indian cultural centres in Ontario cooperated during Ontario's bicentennial to showcase Native music, art, cuisine and theatre. Carl worked with other island artists such as Leland Bell to complete a 12 foot by 40 foot mural for the occasion. Blurry newspaper photos of the day (Manitoulin Recorder, July 17, 1984) show Carl shaking hands with an executive of the E.B. Eddy forest manufacturing company of Espanola during a cheque presentation to the Native festival. At that time the forestry giant had been trying to improve its public image after effluent from the Espanola paper plant had killed fish in the Spanish River. As he accepts the $2000 donation from the mega corporation, Carl looks straight at the camera.

That penetrating gaze has become very familiar to viewers over the years since many of his most compelling works are essentially self-portraits. In galleries from Ottawa to Vancouver, spectators find the teasing, sometimes defiant eyes of the artist following them as they move through the exhibit. And since Carl often expressed many environmental concerns, one can only guess what his thoughts were as he accepted the E.B. Eddy cheque, "in the spirit of sharing."

Early in his career he chose the self-portrait as an effective vehicle for political and environmental commentary. It is likely that his university studies in art history exposed him to other artists who used first person art forms to analyse their own identity and values. His portraits often allude to European artists who were firmly entrenched in the Western canon. For example, Vincent van Gogh (1853-1890), the tormented Dutch painter, was preoccupied with his own image for years. In *Self-portrait with Grey Felt Hat* (1887), the unsmiling artist sports a red beard, white shirt, suit and tie, topped off by a grey hat with an upturned brim. He looks off to the side instead of directly at the viewer.

Unlike van Gogh, Carl chose to make eye contact with his audience. This unblinking stance is apparent when he looks out from a piece entitled *Burying the Ruler #1.* In this 1991 work we witness Carl standing shirtless, clad in blue jeans, sandals and a fedora hat. In his right hand he holds a seemingly mundane wooden ruler, the type one would find in a one-room rural school house or the kind used for punishment in the Garnier residential facility. Some observers have speculated that the ruler symbolizes the European obsession with dominating nature and other cultures. Perhaps it represents the Western tendency towards linear thinking which worships scientific method and precise measurement of everything.

Certainly art history courses are replete with self-portraits by America's Andy Warhol, Mexico's Frida Kahlo and Europe's Rembrandt and Pablo Picasso. For someone with Carl's well-honed sense of parody, it was natural for him to poke fun at the long-established tradition and use it for his own purposes. He would go on to lampoon many sacred cows during his career.

Carl returned to this concept again in 1995, with *Self-portrait 'burying the ruler...'* In this mixed media work we again see the artist standing alone with the image of a beehive outlined below him. In this work, as in many others, he uses beehives to convey the idea that European colonizers were over industrious, hierarchical and came with a sting.

Throughout his lifetime Carl frequently satirized the self-portrait convention with tongue-in-cheek bravado. Take his *Self-portrait in my Christian Dior Bathing Suit* (1980), for instance. This mocking image inspired many other First Nations artists to challenge mainstream assumptions on what constitutes "Indian art" and to explore new ways to express Native identity.

As critic Patricia Vervoort has commented in her essay, entitled, "A Visual Autobiography", the artist examines himself in connection to politics, the environment, history and family. Like other students of his work, she suggests that the images are not solely self-portraits; they are tools to convey his personal statements about art, history and identity.

Dissatisfied with the art establishment, Carl searched for and invented his own personal system of symbols, icons and signs to express his political and spiritual views. He appropriated whatever was necessary to elucidate his concerns about degradation of the environment and the greediness of Western capitalism. For example, he collected material from newspaper articles, text books, archival records and family albums. In some cases, he shredded bank notes into his handmade paper process in order to demonstrate the materialism rampant in the world.

Images of explorers such as Christopher Columbus, figure prominently in his work. Carl's objection to the European version of history prompted him to re-visit that fateful day when the Italian born Spanish navigator made landfall in America. The contact between European and Indigenous people October 12, 1492, escalated the relentless colonization of the western hemisphere. For the original peoples, it meant the death of millions from war, forced labour and disease. These tragic outcomes are commemorated in *The Columbus Boat,* exhibited at The Power Plant, Toronto, 1992. In addition, he used photos of well-known First Nations and Western leaders with a variety of other historical images and his own recurring self-portrait to rewrite history in the *Columbus Suite*.

Anthropology also comes under the Carl Beam microscope. In one of his prints he used a photo depicting pioneer ethnologist Frank Cushing (1857-1900), leading two Zuni Pueblo natives on a tour of "civilized society." Cushing made his reputation when he lived among the Zuni people and became an intimate participant in their culture. He studied their daily lives, listened to their myths and sketched their secret ceremonies. In published journals such as, "My Adventures in Zuni," he popularized his belief in the reciprocal sharing of cultures. Under Carl's scrutiny, it becomes evident that anthropologists play a large role in perpetuating the image of the Indian as ethnographic curiosity.

The sepia toned portraits preserved by frontier photographer Edward S. Curtis (1868-1952), are also referenced as Carl addressed caricatures of "the noble savage" in popular culture. Nicknamed "the shadow catcher," by the people he photographed between 1907 and 1930, Curtis documented the marriage, birth and death rituals of more than eighty tribes. He amassed a collection of 2200 photogravures, plus thousands of pages of text cataloguing Native customs related to dwellings, food, dance and religion. In his view, he was capturing the knowledge of a vanishing race. His ubiquitous images continue to support the romanticized version of the American West so prevalent on this continent.

Since Carl received his early education in a Catholic residential school, it is not surprising to see a profusion of Christian imagery in his work. He was drawn to images of many different types of martyrs or self-sacrificers through the ages. *Forced Ideas in School Days* (1991), contains the melange of past and current persecution that often occupied his mind. It features a residential school class picture with the artist's face circled. Below that is a nod to Renaissance artist, Andrea Mantegna (1431-1506), an Italian painter, engraver and sculptor famous for a canvas called *Dead Christ*. Balancing the crucifixion scene, is an image of an Apache healer.

It is interesting to note that *The Pieta* (pity in Italian), emerged as a recurring image in his collages. The marble sculpture fashioned by Michelangelo (1498), depicts the Virgin Mary cradling the dead body of Jesus in her lap after the crucifixion. He frequently reproduces Jesus on the cross accompanied by two thieves who were crucified with him.

In a piece entitled, *Summa 2*, Carl depicts a whale swimming along the top with the widely disseminated image of Osama bin Laden peering out from behind bars at the bottom. The viewer is reminded that the knowledge of other belief systems, such as Islam, is essentially incomplete or distorted. Throughout history, religion has been the source of conflict and competing ideologies. The reference to *Summa Theologica*, by Thomas Aquinas (1225-1274), tells us that Carl was certainly grappling with ultimate questions. The *Summa* was considered the greatest theological statement of the Middle Ages. Aquinas set out to compile all the theological teachings of the time and to provide an outline for the meaning of life. To initiate beginners into Christian doctrine, the tome included topics such as God's Creation, Man's Purpose, Christ and the Sacraments. Of course, the work was never completed, but perhaps it appealed to Carl because of the interrogative style of the document. As an artist, he continually posed theological, philosophical and spiritual questions through his work.

These concerns are echoed again in *Summa 2, or Still Waiting for Godot (2001) and Beckett.* Why did the Theatre of the Absurd capture Carl's interest? At first glance, an Irish Protestant writer such as Samuel Beckett would seem to have little in common with a Native artist from Canada. Closer inspection, however, reveals some kinship in their creative processes. In plays such as, *Waiting for Godot*, Beckett created a world where unhappy characters battled exploitation and oppression in their ongoing struggle to express themselves. The people in his stories were often alienated, bereft of hope and labouring under an overwhelming burden of grief. Beckett dispensed with conventional theatre techniques and invented his own mode of presentation.

Certainly, this bold approach would have intrigued Carl, as he too was attempting to free himself of stereotypes and alter mainstream ways of thinking. In many of his paintings he employed absurd juxtaposition to stir up both intellectual debate and emotional catharsis. Of course, both were very fond of sarcasm and irony to get their points across. And both left their creations open to a variety of interpretations by the viewing public.

The giants of the Western scientific community also appeared in Carl's work juxtaposed with portraits of Aboriginal leaders. For instance, he had a particular fascination with Albert Einstein (1879-1955), the German theoretical physicist whose name is synonymous with the word, genius. Einstein published the "theory of relativity" and won the "Nobel Prize for Physics" (1921). For Carl, however, the renowned intellect of the nuclear age might have served as a symbol of bad science. Nuclear disasters such as Three Mile Island and Chernobyl, were very much on his mind. Works such as *Albert in the Blue Box* and *Einstein and Sitting Bull* (1991), ask viewers to question the supremacy of scientific thinking and to honour other paths to wisdom.

Sitting Bull (1831-1890), a Sioux leader and prophet, is commemorated in many of Carl's mixed media pieces. For North Americans he has long symbolized bravery, insight, integrity and defiance. When the United States government tried to forcibly confine his people on reservations, Sitting Bull resisted. In 1876, he took part in an inter-tribal attack on Col. George Armstrong Custer at the Battle of Little Bighorn. Although he fled to safety in Canada after the battle, he was lured back across the border with the promise of amnesty in 1881. However, he was viewed as an instigator and spent two years in a US prison. Sitting Bull and his followers did not passively accept the annexing of their land; clashes with reservation police led to the death of the intractable chief and a dozen of his supporters in 1890.

Carl was undoubtedly impressed with Sitting Bull's unflinching gaze at the camera in those vintage photographs. According to historical archives, the visionary Tatanka-Iyotanka had always warned his people to be wary of white society and Christianity. He always rebelled against confinement of any kind. It is easy to understand why Carl would invoke the spirit of Sitting Bull to reinforce his message.

Carl's own personal journey did not follow a linear path. He travelled extensively with his wife Ann and daughter Anong, and lived in the American Southwest in the 1980s. However, he always returned to his Manitoulin roots. In the 1990s, they brought a little taste of New Mexico to M'Chigeeng when they built an adobe house designed to withstand Northern Ontario's winters.

Manitoulin residents will also remember Carl's generosity in the summer of 2004, when he helped the Manitoulin Fine Arts Association celebrate its tenth anniversary during a symposium held at the Ojibwe Cultural Foundation. He shared his perspectives in a workshop entitled, "Empower Your Art," a session designed to teach some of the lessons he felt were neglected in formal art schools. During the July 2 reception, he also delivered a slide show and lecture entitled, "A Post-Modern Approach to Art Making."

"In the past, Native art was not seen as contemporary art. A lot of Native art is still undiscovered," he told his Manitoulin audience.

In the same address, he poked fun at himself, saying, most people expect his art to always convey a serious wake-up call for the public. “I am not always expressing a political agenda,” he smiled. “Sometimes the work is just a good composition or an appealing harmony of colour.”

He acknowledged that viewers often feel compelled to discuss his themes or to decipher a profound meaning from the work.

“Generally, the prime objective is to do something interesting and colourful for our fellow citizens,” he said. “Some of my paintings may have incidental meaning, a meaning I did not intend. People do tend to read into my work, but I am all in favour of a free sharing of an idea with others.”

Carl Beam left behind a series of meditations on self, history and possibility. His works are not meant for the lazy or the complacent viewer. They are not simplistic or easy to comprehend. He urged people not to absorb and accept the cultural signs imposed upon them. In his own life’s work he attempted to change society by changing the meaning of cultural signs. He didn’t just re-code the signals of the dominant society; he created new ones.

In many ways, Carl was a modern hip-hop artist, a free flowing rapster sampling, borrowing, appropriating and collecting whatever he needed to convey his messages. Along the way he would often revisit themes and mix and re-mix for refinement and clarification.

His work remains an enduring plea for humans to look more closely at how they see things, at how they live their lives and at how they often repeat the ills and wrongs of the past.

His wife Ann Beam believes her partner of twenty five years made a lasting impact on the Canadian art scene. “Carl Beam was one of the greatest artists that this country has ever produced,” she stated. “It is really good to see his work getting the acknowledgement and attention it truly deserves. There are young people in colleges and universities now, encountering his work in their curriculum, who are thrilled to discover that he was an Aboriginal man and that he lived and worked in Canada and made such amazing art.”

ANN BEAM (1944 -):
Taking time to listen to the holy buzz

When Ann Beam meets you at the door of her home, she may be carrying an arm load of wood for one of the two stoves that keep her adobe house cosy on those frigid February nights on Manitoulin. Or she may be putting the finishing touches on a raven or eagle motif for one of her unique ceramic pieces. If you are lucky, she will have time for tea and a chat about her current projects and her upcoming exhibitions.

A conversation may meander from the mundane and the practical to the ethereal and the spiritual as her two watchful dogs slumber quietly nearby. In this calming atmosphere the sun dapples through the window sending crystal rainbows over the carpets, the canvases and the cupboards. Hanging from the rafters are clusters of dried maize and huge sunflower heads ready to burst with seeds. On an antique hutch in the corner, found objects, art supplies and family photos are clustered together in a riot of cross-pollination.

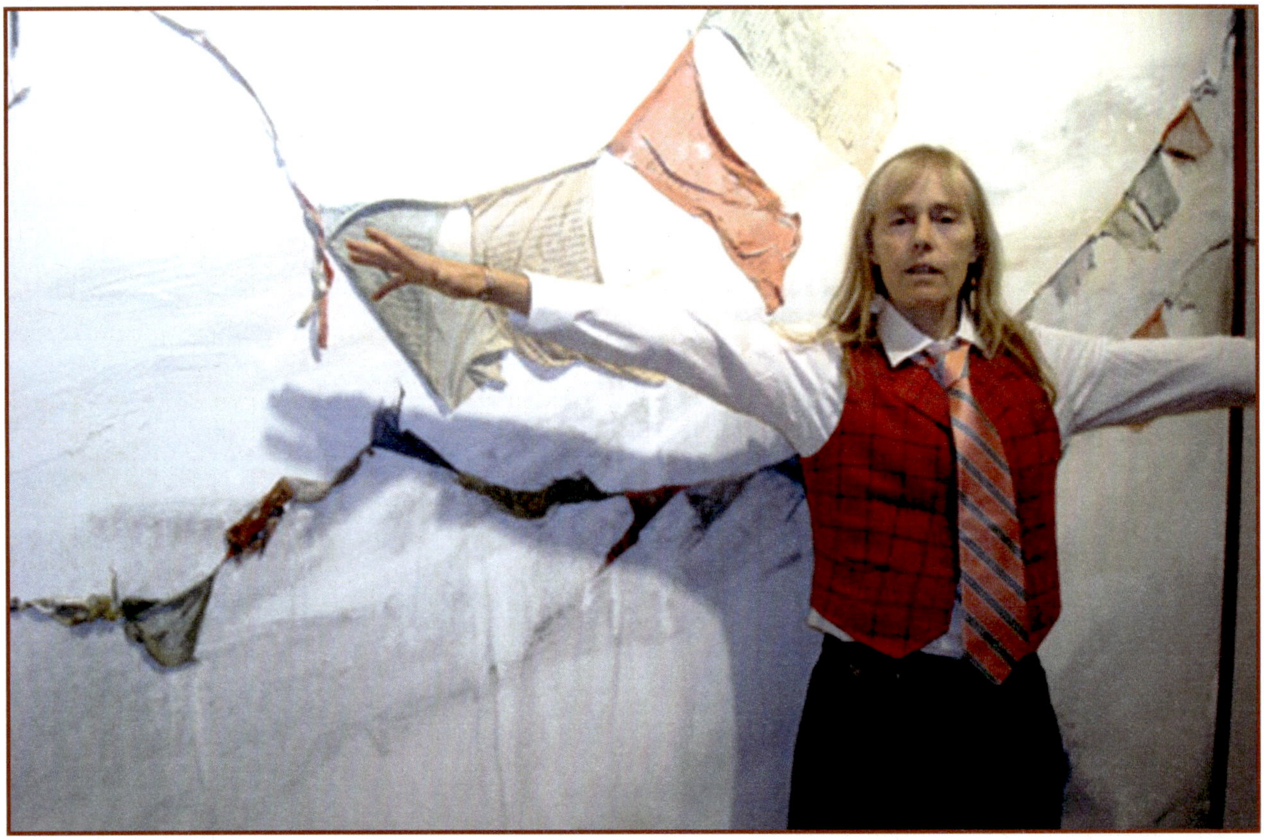

Although Manitoulin Island has become the centre of the Universe for her now, Ann has travelled to many extraordinary places and has immersed herself in many extraordinary experiences before putting down roots. At this writing, she continues to refine and expand a forty year art practice focussing on ceramics, painting, printmaking and book design.

As a child, raised by adoptive parents in New Jersey and Brooklyn, her creative spirit was always evident. After high school, she completed her Bachelor of Fine Arts at the State University of New York, in Buffalo (1968). As she grew older, she was drawn to research her family of origin and rediscover her Cherokee/Celtic heritage. All of this rich cultural inheritance infuses her life and surfaces in distinctive motifs in her painting, weaving, writing and sculpting.

Like many other conscientious objectors before her, Ann moved north of the border in the 1960s, to escape the pervasive military atmosphere in the United States.

"I came to Canada because I was attracted by the cosmopolitan nature of Toronto," she said. "It was so shockingly clean back then. I was quite politicized as a young woman; I didn't want my tax dollars used to support the conflict in Viet Nam."

The 1970s were a productive time for Ann, as she found many outlets for her artistic talents. She went to work as director for Kids Can Press in 1976 and she experimented with etching and lithography at the Open Studio in Toronto from 1974 to 1978. In addition, she exhibited her work at the Pollack Gallery and in the "Chair Show" at the Art Gallery of Ontario (AGO) in Toronto. She did a stint as an editorial artist at the Toronto Star and taught classes at the AGO. Within twelve years, she had met her life partner, Carl Beam, and became adept at juggling the roles of artist, wife and mother. They would go on to spend a quarter of a century travelling, painting, building and working together. Ann describes this time as "a great adventure" which deepened her as a person and deepened her art as well.

"I am living in the house we built together so he's referenced all the time in my heart and mind," she acknowledged. "We had a continuous running dialogue on the principles of art and life over twenty six years together. And our daughter, Anong inhaled the dialogue as she grew up."

The Neon Raven Gallery, established by the Beam family in M'Chigeeng, has developed a loyal clientele. Although businesses of all types in North America faltered in the aftermath of the 9/11 terrorist attacks in New York (2001), arts related enterprises struggled more than most.

In her view, many artists survive at the subsistence level because many Canadians still consider art a frill and are reluctant to purchase what they consider to be luxury items.

"Art is a continuous enrichment," she said. "It imports ongoing benefits for the viewer. When you buy artwork that is meaningful, it is like investing in yourself."

And yet she doesn't let public misconceptions distract her from her mission. She strives to balance the creative calling with the practicalities of marketing.

"In 2007, we had our best year ever at the gallery and that encouraged me. I may have had second thoughts at first, but now I see that the visitors will come. And I do enjoy meeting the people and seeing how they are inspired by the art."

Winter brings the solitude needed to stoke the fires of the imagination. It's the perfect time to court the Muse and to be open to new directions, new imagery. For Ann, the excitement of starting a new project never wanes. As she opens a fresh shipment of fine tinted watercolour paper from Montreal, she is already anticipating the way it will receive the energy of the paint.

"Winter is a good time to get back to the heart of the art," she said. "It's a good time to stay connected to the holy buzz that feeds your art. It's a spiritual thing and you need to honour it and follow it."

A 40"x30" watercolour entitled, *Lift*, provides a glimpse into her personal quest to rededicate herself and to step forward into a new level of her art practice. The painting depicts an expansive scallop shell suspended over a diminutive image of Ann herself. She is surrounded by the hard-baked stone of ancient ruins located at Chaco Canyon three hours out of Albuquerque, in the northwest quadrant of New Mexico. Here, the prehistoric Anasazi people had built a civilization that lasted from 900 to 1130 AD. The Pueblo people constructed road networks, irrigation systems, great corn silos and sophisticated solar and lunar calendars. A very artistic culture, they were famous for their pottery. Although the culture mysteriously disappeared, the site is still regarded as a magic place where watchful spirits still preside over the cliffs and tablelands of sun-bleached sandstone. Ann and Carl Beam were drawn to this special place in November 1999.

"It's just before the new millennium," she confided. "I'm in a ceremonial kiva. The canyon is cool and the shadows are long. I can see all the little dark windows of the kiva all around me; I can feel the guardian spirits observing me."

In respect and reverence, she presented water and tobacco to the old spirits.

"They saw me and they accepted my offering," she recalled. "I presented myself on stage and I was lifted; they ignited my heart. It's a spiritual thing to step up to the plate and to take responsibility for the gifts you have been given. I knew I had to move forward. I was going to do what I was brought here to do."

Since the new millennium, and her uplifting experience at the kiva, Ann has been transformed into a self-described "receiver dish" open to patterns in the environment and synchronous events in the world. Gradually she has become fully attuned to "the holy buzz" and conscious of symbols and objects that speak to her. During one particularly prolific period, her attention was centred on archetypal shell imagery, as evidenced by her collection of shells of all sizes and shapes gathered from her extensive travels.

"Shells have always been important to the original cultures," she pointed out. "Many cultures have revered them as powerful objects. This connection to Shell goes back a long time with me and its imagery connects me deeply to who I am, where I've been and where I'm going."

When she is in a highly productive phase, she works on several projects simultaneously. In recent years, she has created a series of "medicine boxes" containing shells, traditional medicines and other natural objects as well as ceramic pieces and installations.

"It is important for people to find things in the world that inspire them. I am inspired by the radiant nature of light and energy," she explained. "It can be human or an object; it can be organic or inorganic. Light energy passes through everything. When you look at the scallop shell, for instance, you can see how the radiant structure moves from a point. The energy that went through is recorded in the calcium."

As she develops her own distinctive "shell theory," she makes playful references to the eternal gap that exists between the humanities and science. As she juxtaposes shells with humans and planet earth, she is well aware that scientists, such as Isaac Newton, used shell theory to analyse planetary motion. In classical mechanics, the shell theorem gives gravitational simplifications which can be applied to objects inside or outside a spherically symmetrical body. For example, Newton showed that a spherically symmetric body affects external objects gravitationally as though all of its mass were concentrated at a point at its centre. However, Ann is more fascinated by the gravitational circumstances of the heart and what weighs upon it.

"I like to take scientific notions and drag them across their bifurcated reality (kicking and screaming), to their denied sister, the Ancient Sciences," she said. "There is no hard edge there between Spirit and Matter."

She has elaborated on the belief that shells are "power-filled," in a series of watercolours which pair shells with self-portraits, healing plants and images from newspaper headlines. In a work entitled, *Shamans and Shell*, two Ecuadoran medicine people are crouched close to the ground while a massive scallop shell is suspended above them in a dark sky. The male shaman mixes medicine in a large pottery bowl while his female companion sits protectively behind him and gazes off into the distance.

The shamans are engaged in a struggle to save "the vine of the soul" (also known as Ayahuasca) from the control of multi-national pharmaceutical corporations, according to the artist. The sacred plant has always been revered for its extraordinary visionary and healing powers by the peoples of the Amazon. Indigenous healers have been fighting to keep commercial enterprises from patenting the drug and violating the traditional practices.

"I have been drawn to the scallop shell because I see it as a spiritually expansive image," she elaborated. "It's like a protractor; it fans out like a person with her arms up and her hands out. It's like an open heart; it's synonymous with a sunrise."

This uplifting sensation is also present in a work she calls *Shell and the Letter a*. Again the curvaceous seashell fans out across the canvas encouraging an upward movement of heart and mind.

Similarly, the shell exerts its positive energy on this fragile planet in a work fittingly named *Earth and Shell*. As Ann contemplates the state of the world, she is confronted with so many "heartbreaking phenomena," that she feels compelled to create soothing imagery and balm for the spirit.

"It's my artist's effort to calm the spirit of Mother Earth because of all the challenges she faces, because of all the things we have done to her," Ann said. "She's heavily stressed."

In *Shiites and Shells*, grey scallop shapes encircle a group of Shiite women huddled in the centre of the canvas. One of the shells is shaded black to echo the black robes of the women moving across the desert. Although the artist generally avoids direct political commentary in her work, it is instructive to remember that historically Shiite women have been doubly oppressed, by their husbands and by their political rulers in Muslim countries. The historical strife between Sunni and Shiite sects has been well-documented in Western media reports. The religious feuding has led to many deaths in Iraq. Undoubtedly it would take a strong circle of shells to calm the spirit of these troubled lands.

Most of Ann's paintings have strong evocative titles, but an image of Palestinian leader, Yasser Arafat (1929-2004), supported by a dozen seashells remains "untitled." Instead, the artist has excerpted a chapter from a medical text that focuses on "substances that calm the spirit." Again the artist refrains from taking sides in age-old conflicts; viewers are free to make their own interpretation.

With war raging on many fronts around the world, it is time to pause and reflect, Ann believes. Through her work she is intent on promoting life affirming ideas and creating a ripple effect of positive change.

"We need to get anchored," she suggested. "We need to get hold of ourselves and calm down and see where we really want to go. I believe we are all connected. We are even connected to the people making bad decisions whether we like it or not. They are part of us. I'm offering good thoughts here in my art; I believe that when we offer good thoughts, it has a profound impact on the world. Now is a pivotal time in our collective history when we can change things with our best thoughts and our best intentions."

But, for real change to take place, humans must begin to listen to one another and listen to the cries of distress from Nature, her works suggest. In another self-portrait labelled *Cochlea*, Ann stands beside a large conch shell with an illustration of the auditory portion of the inner ear positioned on top. Since the cochlea looks like a spiral-shaped snail shell it is an apt vehicle for advancing her "shell theory." Also in keeping with this theme, a depiction of the human ear and the snail-like cochlea nestles close to the Earth in a watercolour entitled, *Ear Hear Earth Heart*. The viewer is invited to listen to the sound of creation and the heartbeat of Mother Earth.

Always a staunch protector of the environment and advocate for natural medicines, Ann has given Earth a prominent position in many of her paintings. The planet's corona accompanies images of shamans, shells and orchids among others.

"The aura of the Earth resonates with me personally," she said. "In all the images I do now, the Earth is always present. It's still a rapture for me to paint the Earth because the Earth is a living, spiritual being that is accommodating our human development."

This respect for nature's wisdom has guided her studies of healing plants and the traditional remedies used in older cultures. She has been particularly fascinated with aspects of the *Materia Medica*, the body of collected knowledge about the therapeutic properties of any substance used for healing. In the course of her research, she has turned her attention to a chapter devoted to substances which calm the spirit. Herbs and other substances that anchor and settle the spirit are showcased throughout her body of work.

"The fact that spirit is alluded to at all in a book about medicine is pretty exciting," she noted. "Contemporary western allopathic medicine leaves it out of the picture completely. The substances that calm the spirit are primarily bones and shells."

To illustrate their power to soothe, Ann has been known to gather many treasured items from her own personal collection and arrange them in a large sandbox during her art exhibitions. Deer bones and clam shells from Manitoulin mingle with bones from New Mexico and assorted shells from Florida in an open medicine box.

Fans of her work expect to find medicine boxes of various sizes in her gallery and public exhibits. Most of these compact but powerful spiritual first-aid kits are designed to provide much needed therapy for a stressed planet or for a racing human heart. For example, in *Medicine Box 4*, the artist has placed a bottle of Dr. Bach's Rescue Remedy next to an image of Earth. The Angel Gabriel hovers protectively over a plastic bottle of water in *Essential Relationship* (Medicine Box 10.) And a fragile moth is superimposed on a full moon in a former cigar box converted to Medicine Box 9. Perhaps the most imposing of this series is a large glassed in enclosure featuring Earth buoyed up by a massive collection of abalone shells, long considered sacred objects by First Nations.

As with all art, literary or visual, it is inappropriate to impose too many personal interpretations on the work. The themes and the images emerge from an intuitive source unique to the artist.

"It's important not to dissect it too much," Ann said. "It's not good to over analyse things. I work with images that I feel compelled to work with through a type of searching or inspiration. The intent, loosely speaking, would be to uplift the hearts and minds of the people of this Earth."

If her higher purpose is to alter perspectives and promote tolerance, then a 7'x9' canvas entitled, *High Altitude Prayer*, succeeds on many levels. In the painting, the Earth is almost completely shrouded in dense cloud cover. Only a small patch of the blue planet is visible through the blanket of white and grey. High above the receding world three chorus lines of prayer cloths dance across the canvas. Although somewhat frayed by buffeting wind and faded by pelting rain, the multi-hued prayer flags keep flying in an upward motion. Sailing like errant kites above the Earth, they encircle the globe with uplifting messages of hope and comfort.

"Across the board, this has been the most generally accepted painting I've ever done," she mused. "Everyone understands it; they actually love it. It works for them no matter what culture they are from. It expresses sentiments similar to the Native American feather prayer."

Since 2000, Ann's innovative work has spoken to an even larger audience and received widespread appreciation. Overseas her works were exhibited at the Novak Graphics Studio in Shanghai, China (2001) and at the Orfield Gallery in Minneapolis, Minnesota (2006-2007). Canadian shows included "Picturing Her: Images of Girlhood" at the McCord Museum in Montreal, Quebec (2005-2006), "Motherlines" at Carleton University Gallery, Ottawa, Ontario (2004) and "Shamans and Ravens" at the DeLeon White Gallery, Toronto, Ontario (2002). In addition, she had a solo exhibition entitled "Sub-Division Suite/Earth Builders' Narrative" at the Strutts Gallery, Sackville, New Brunswick (2000). On Manitoulin Island the Sheguiandah Museum hosted her "Corona, Dialogues with Mother Earth," in 2005. "Earth and Shell," ran at the Gore Bay Museum from mid-August to mid-October 2008. And, of course, throughout her career there have been many group shows as well as collaborative exhibitions with husband Carl and daughter Anong.

Although visual art has been the primary medium for grappling with political and social concerns, Ann has expressed herself in literary forms as well. She issued *At the Animal Dance* in 1980, with 32 colour lithographs and again in a trade edition in 2000. In 2006, she brought her compassion and understated humour to focus on addiction issues. The independently published children's book entitled, *The Bear's Breakthrough/ Makwa Gaa Zhaapshkang*, recognizes that youngsters need messages of hope during troubling times. In this lavishly illustrated publication, she tells the story of one particular bear who loved beer pancakes so much they were having "a deleterious effect" on his health. Fortunately, the bear is surrounded by people who care deeply. Unconditional love and faith become the key ingredients in the recipe for the bear's salvation. The tale serves as a salutary potion for all creatures who have "some hurts that need healing."

The Mouse Came to My House/Waabgonoojiinhs Gii Dagoshin Endaa'ahn, published in English and Ojibwe, was released in 2008. Accompanied by Ann's own whimsical illustrations, the compassionate and gentle tale reinforces many of the artist's unwavering convictions. Essentially, we are all connected; an injury to one is an injury to all, and we need to find creative ways to live in harmony with our fellow inhabitants of the planet.

And so the seasons pass at the Neon Raven gallery and dark gives way to light. Ann Beam continues her mission to silence the chatter of the rational mind and listen for the "holy buzz," as she strives for new ways to work her artist's magic and to touch the heart.

ANONG MIGWANS BEAM (1980 -)

From the moment of her birth in 1980, Anong Migwans Beam has been surrounded by the sights, sounds, smells and tastes of the working artist's studio. As the child of two professional artists, her formative years were spent listening and learning as Carl and Ann Beam nurtured her curious mind with new vistas and fresh ideas. While she was growing up, it seemed perfectly natural to be immersed in such a stimulating environment.

"My parents dedicated themselves fully to art," she recalled. "I never observed them have so-called regular jobs. I didn't see anything unusual about it."

She absorbed the innate creativity that permeated the Beam household no matter where they lived on Turtle Island.

"My parents always had sketchbooks available for me," she said. "They always got excited about drawing with me. I remember I had a Pelican watercolour set, a double decker box of colours that I enjoyed painting with. At that time I was painting a lot of geometric designs and I also liked doing drawings of princesses."

With the passage of time, she has developed an even greater appreciation of the gifts she has inherited. "I have always respected the fact that they did just art and didn't have regular jobs. One of the best things I learned from them was my inquisitiveness. I can always find things to devote resources to and to learn and to explore."

Although her parents made creative materials readily available for her to indulge her imagination, Anong never felt there was pressure to follow in their footsteps. Instead, they were content to expose her to diverse landscapes and interesting journeys throughout her childhood. Now, as an adult with her own solo art career, she looks back at these early adventures with great fondness.

"When I was a toddler, we spent some time in New Mexico," she related. "And when I was age three, we relocated to Peterborough, Ontario. I would sometimes accompany my Dad when he went to speak at various art conferences as well. One of our most memorable trips was when we were in Europe and took a train to Paris with a group of Native artists. We also went to the Netherlands when I was five and visited Ann Frank's house."

It was not unusual for the Beams to embark on road trips that would take them to places such as the American Southwest or to British Columbia. But by 1992, they were putting down firmer roots on Manitoulin Island. During this period they built the unique adobe structures in M'Chigeeng that would house their home and gallery.

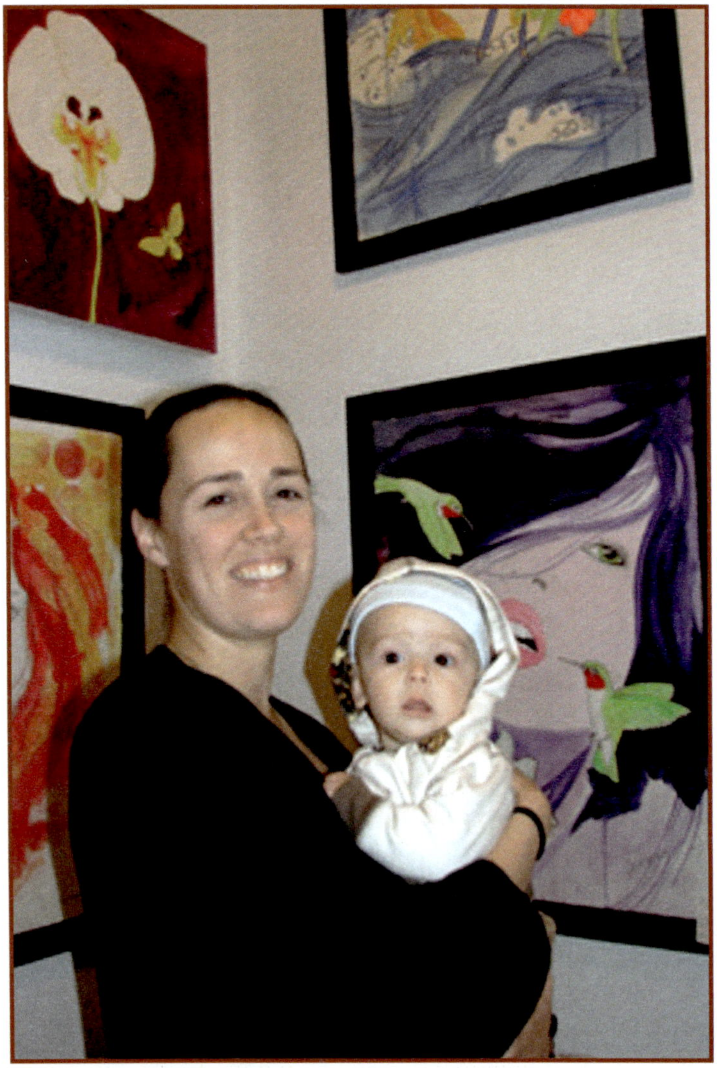

During her years in Manitoulin schools, Anong's vocational aspirations were not confined exclusively to art. Since she had been raised in an atmosphere of few boundaries, she wasn't one to impose limits on herself. In fact, as a youngster she had considered the lofty goal of becoming Canadian prime minister one day. Later, around the age of twelve, she was drawn to the field of ethno-botany. But even as she examined these possibilities, the art was still calling to her.

A conversation with her father shortly before graduation helped her weigh her options and gain some perspective on the opportunities available to a young woman with eclectic interests. "He told me to think about my quality of life in choosing a career path," she said. "He pointed out that professionals like lawyers and doctors get up early and put in long hours on the job. However, being an artist offers freedom of choice. When you are an artist, you can set your own schedule and you can live a much more unique kind of life."

In retrospect, Anong has been able to appreciate the wisdom inherent in that advice. She now accepts that being an artist is in many ways more demanding than a regimented nine to five occupation.

"It is much more intensive than being a regular worker because there's more travel involved, more searching for materials and a whole different set of challenges and demands," she noted.

When she finally made up her mind to attend art school, she wanted to make sure it would be truly "engaging." Thus her decision to opt for the School of the Museum of Fine Arts in Boston, in 1998. She complemented that visual arts program with further studies at the Ontario College of Art and Design (1999-2000). She also attended the Institute of American Indian Arts in 2001.

In art school she discovered that many of her fellow students were ardent fans of her father's work. They admired the way he battled the status quo in art and they were eager to emulate him.

As she explored her own personal themes and various media, she participated in several group shows including the 1999 "Symbolic Woman" exhibit at the Michael Price Gallery, in Boston. The New Millennium kicked off an inspiring period for Anong as she took part in "First Nations Art 2000," at the Woodland Cultural Centre in Brantford, Ontario and the "Time Before Memory" show, featuring the Native Students Association at the Ontario Academy of Art and Design (OCAD) in Toronto. That same year she was featured in the "Novak Graphics Print Show," in Shen-Zhen and Shanghai, China as well as the "Landscape" exhibit at the Praxis Gallery, Toronto. The Propeller Gallery has also showcased her work.

The following year, she contributed works to Toronto shows entitled, "Red Millennium" at OCAD and "Contact" at the Edward Day Gallery. In December 2001, she participated in "Untold/Retold", a juried student show at the IAIA Museum, Santa Fe.

With growing confidence, she exhibited selected works at the Steel City Gallery in Hamilton, Ontario in 2002. That spring she also submitted work to the "Verses" show at the IAIA.

By 2003, she and husband Mark Larochelle had settled down on Manitoulin not far from her parents. She continued to experiment with drawing, painting, photography and ceramics. The ceramic work began to take centre stage at this time since the entire Beam family had been working with clay for many years.

It seemed a natural progression for Carl, Ann and Anong to join forces and exhibit their ceramic pieces together. The show entitled, "It's All Relative," travelled from the Canadian Clay and Glass Gallery, in Waterloo, to other sites in Ontario including, the Art Gallery of Algoma, the Thunder Bay Art Gallery and the Agnes Jamieson Art Gallery in Minden.

"I first learned to do ceramics at the age of five," she said. "I have been doing it my whole life. It was really great to be showing ceramics with my Mom and Dad. It was really exciting."

"It's All Relative" showcased Anong's Asian-inspired ceramic platters, pots, jars and cups. In an essay accompanying the exhibition catalogue, Virginia MacDonnell Eichhorn described her work as "calm and gracious" and praised the harmonious and understated quality of the pieces.

Despite the positive reviews, Anong does not consider herself primarily a ceramicist. She experiments with a wide range of creative endeavours, including writing and recording music with her husband. Their versatility has led them to innovative collaborations with musicians internationally. And in 2008, the couple established an Ojibway language radio station in M'Chigeeng First Nation.

Motherhood has added a new dimension to Anong's outlook and work. The birth of Riel Migwans Beam Larochelle on her father's birthday in 2008, inspired further reflections on the enduring legacy of her father/mentor.

"I have benefited a lot from the freedom my Dad created," she concluded. "He came from a generation of artists who made it possible to break free of stereotypes. It's a real luxury for me to just be an artist and not just an Native artist. I am free to create outside of expected stereotypes. He spent his entire career fighting against those assumptions."

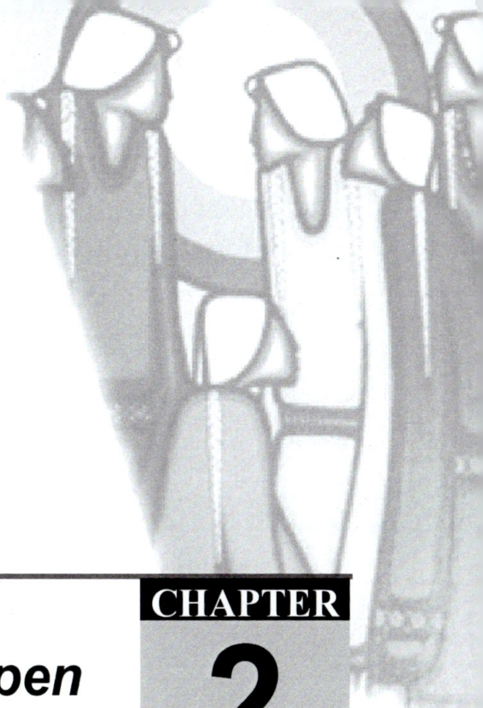

DR. LELAND BELL (1953 -): One Who Talks Honestly in an Open Way of Truth

CHAPTER 2

Step softly as you enter Leland Bell's art gallery. You might just find a snoozing Siamese cat stretched out in a pool of sunlight just inside the entranceway. The restful repose of the studio feline is the first sign of the warm and peaceful atmosphere within.

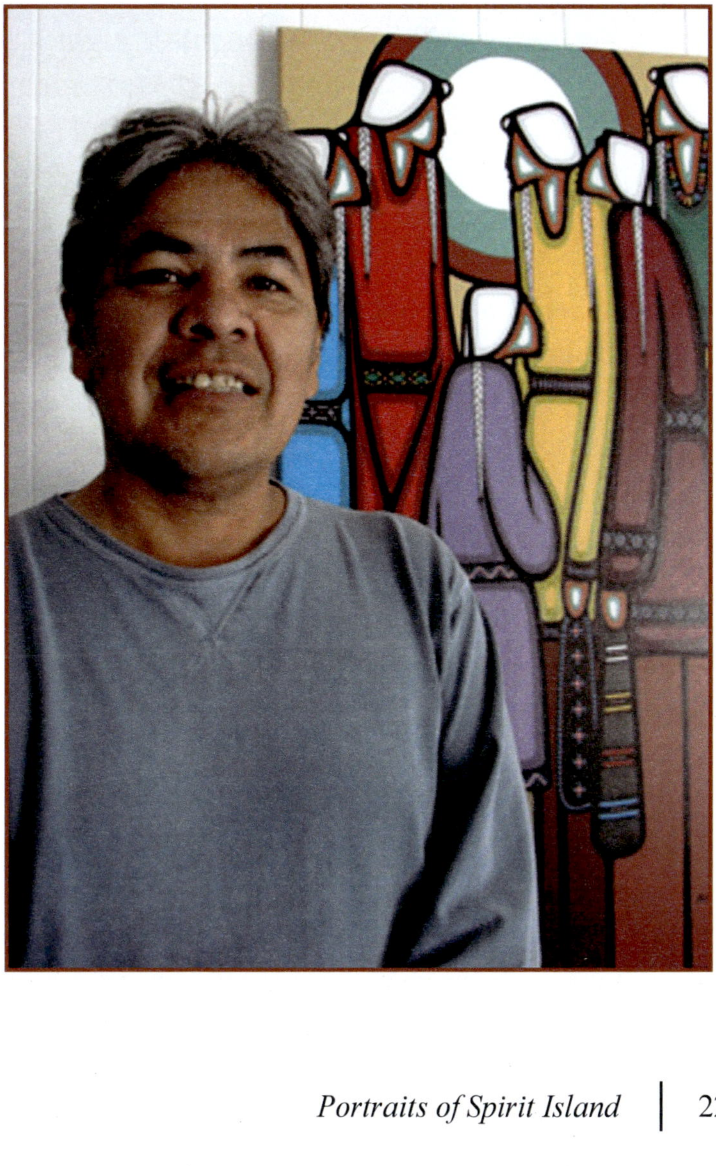

Visitors arrive from the four directions to discover for the first time or to renew an acquaintance with Bebaminojmat, a celebrated Anishinaabe artist, musician and writer. Over the past thirty years, Leland's powerful imagery has been embraced by religious and educational institutions, government agencies, gallery owners and private collectors. His original and iconic works are familiar throughout North America and Europe.

The uplifting themes in his paintings have struck an universal chord with viewers and have enduring cross-cultural appeal.

On a sweltering hot August day in the midst of a Manitoulin heat wave, Leland retreated to a shady canopy in the yard behind his Eshkibok Road gallery. In a far-ranging conversation, he shared memories of his early years and the adventures that would take him far from his home in Wikwemikong.

Up until age ten, he was raised in a foster home in Wikwemikong. Eventually, however, he had the opportunity to move to Toronto where he lived with his biological mother.

He described the urban experience as both "culture shock and future shock" combined. He grew up fast in the Toronto district known as Cabbagetown. "Every second word in that neighbourhood was a swear word," he laughed.

He struggled with the English language in those days, nevertheless, he had a strong impulse to express himself in a variety of ways. During that period he started writing poetry and songs. At the same time he continued to experiment with sketches as well as oil and pastel work. Both the writing and the painting sustained him in the often uninspiring city. Unfortunately, some of his poetry was lost in a fire.

"Writing my little poems in grade eight was one way to connect to my heritage," he said. "I've always liked music. My first memory of becoming aware of music as a child was when I heard Johnny Cash singing "I Walk the Line."

In Toronto, he attended Castlefrank High School and the Danforth Technical Institute. The city did give him the opportunity to discover the Art Gallery of Ontario and to see the fabled Group of Seven. The abstract mountains prominent in the work of Lawren Harris attracted his attention for a time.

"I didn't think of myself as cultured then," he said. "I had been studying graphic arts not fine arts. Actually, I never liked the term artist and I never applied it to myself for many years. In fact, I rejected the label."

Like many young men at eighteen, he was somewhat restless; he hadn't yet recognized his special gifts or discerned his life's purpose. Then one fateful summer day in the early 1970s, he set out to hitchhike to Chicago, and he landed in a spot of trouble in St. Catharines, Ontario. Fortunately, his sister intervened and convinced him to come home. She suggested he check out a summer art camp being organized by the Manitou Arts Foundation.

"I didn't need to be coaxed too hard," he smiled. "My sister told me that Duke Redbird, Tom Peltier and Frank Meawasige were involved."

Tom Peltier, the organizer, asked him to help out with maintenance, and the rest, as they say, is history.

The organizers invited Native youth from communities all across Ontario to join the unique gathering at Schreiber Island in the North Channel of Lake Huron. The site would later be dubbed 'Spider Island' in tribute to the hairy, long-legged companions in their sleeping quarters. In retrospect, Leland recognized this sojourn as a turning point for him and for many of his contemporaries.

He played a maintenance role in the first year of the camp and was responsible for such mundane chores as "cleaning up the lavatories." But he also spent time "just getting to know people" and meshing with the community of artists. Because he played guitar and other instruments, it was easy for him to fit in and to develop rapport.

"I like to laugh and to be involved in creativity of all kinds. And there were artists there involved in a whole range of artistic expression," he noted. "There were a whole bunch of us from all over the place. It was great to be around young people who were expressing their Anishinaabe identity. There was a lot of interaction among the young people and the artists were all supportive of one another."

It wasn't until the second year of the Schreiber Island event, that Leland got fully involved as an artist. He would form an enduring bond with Blake Debassige and Shirley Cheechoo that would see them collaborate on many creative endeavours over the next few decades.

The venue provided a chance to interact with art students from West Bay, Wikwemikong, Kenora and Six Nations. He recalled meeting Mel Madahbee, Robert Green and Joseph Linklater and being exposed to the work of Carl Ray, Saul Williams and Wikwemikong's own Daphne Odjig.

"My first paintings were kind of psychedelic," he mused. "I was mesmerized by the painting activity itself. That was where I learned to experience this thing called art."

He gained confidence as a writer too. Daphne Odjig's response to his work stayed in his memory and influenced his future conduct.

"I showed her a poem and she paid attention to me. That's where I learned dignity, from her. And I try to practice that in all that I do. When I meet people, I try to treat them with dignity."

He has continued to pay tribute to her as a positive role model for a new generation of First Nations artists. In a 2007 symposium at Laurentian University, he acknowledged her struggles as a trailblazer.

"I am thankful to Daphne; she has done so much work for us so that today we can stand here and be proud. She's like a hero to me."

After the Schreiber Island camps wound down, Leland and some of the other young apprentices attended art classes under the auspices of the Ojibwe Cultural Foundation (OCF). Part of the OCF mandate was to reach out and to nurture Anishinaabe artists. These sessions began in 1976, at beautiful Dreamer's Rock on the Whitefish River First Nation. The site was selected for its historical and spiritual significance. Traditionally, it was a place to receive a vision, a place to receive inspiration for one's future path.

Elders from Manitoulin, Saskatchewan and Manitoba were invited to Birch Island to share their knowledge with the youth.

"At the OCF camps there were always Elders present," Leland said. "They led us in sunrise ceremonies and the sweat lodge. In fact, they always strongly suggested we get up for the sunrise ceremonies," he added with his trademark humour.

The self-discipline paid off. It was as if all the disparate threads of his creativity were integrated in that magical place. It was here that Bebaminojmat discovered the unique style that would guide his brushstrokes from then on.

He was open and receptive to the revelations he would receive at Dreamer's Rock. Earlier, he had dreamed that he would be given gifts, but in the dream, the nature of the gifts was not given in detail. He would have to wait until the time was right.

"I had a beautiful vivid dream that would become the source of my art," he confided. "It is important to keep your dreams to yourself because they give you strength."

Other artists at the OCF summer camp validated his experience and affirmed his perceptions.

"I said Eureka; I have found it; it's what I was looking for. And then Mel Madahbee and Randy Trudeau came around and they said 'that's you.' And so I have been developing that style all these years."

Leland has remained a steadfast supporter of the summer art camp concept as a way to reach wayward teens.

"I think the art camps are very important for young people," he told a 2007 gathering at the OCF in M'Chigeeng. "Even if you get lonely, they bring a lot of life to you and you get the chance to sing Anishinaabe songs and to experience new things."

The relaxed and informal atmosphere at the summer art camps allowed Leland and the other novice artists to explore without pressure.

"There was no teaching or instruction as such," he reminded his listeners. "It was more of a peer learning situation. For example, one person would know how to stretch a canvas and another would know how to mix blue or green or yellow so we would all go to watch."

Away from time-clocks and rigid routines, the fledgling artists followed their own biorhythms. They were allowed to be spontaneous if a drum group or a film crew arrived on site.

"We would paint all day and then someone would come and check on us," he said. "We would go swimming or play guitar and jam in the evenings. Then maybe some of us would paint all night until sunrise. We had the freedom to paint. We threw ideas at each other and we had fun just relating to each other without any strict supervision. You can't help but be influenced by the other artists around you. Of course, at age seventeen you think you know everything, but in the end we learned to find our own unique styles."

In his view, community leaders should continue to provide creative outlets for First Nations youngsters and to provide forums for interaction with mentors.

Over the years, Leland has been asked to address educational forums on many occasions. When he has spoken to youth groups he has always assured them that they will discover their own gifts as they mature. To illustrate, he often joked about his own tentative attempts to try dramatic acting at summer camp. He admitted to suffering stage fright and a tendency to freeze up when it came time for him to say his lines. He couldn't feel comfortable and say his part naturally so he "gave up acting." Fortunately for the community and the art world, he found his comfort zone elsewhere.

Leland has been honing and refining the style he discovered in those stimulating times. Others might have decided to head off to some mainstream academic art college to advance their careers, but that was not his way. In his heart he knew that much of the truth he sought could be found by immersing himself in the culture of his ancestors. He followed the beat of the ancient drum and discovered hope, courage and liberty.

"Our ways were forbidden and went underground for a long, long time, but the Anishinaabe teachings have become an important part of my life," he reiterated. "For me, my spirituality and my art are the same thing."

In childhood he had been taught the tenets of Christianity and had attended some Catholic services, but he found nothing in the Christian doctrine to make him feel comfort, he said. Eventually, he went looking for a better fit.

At age twenty-two, that quest led him to present tobacco to an Elder and to request an Anishinaabe name. After about a year, a naming ceremony was held for him in Wikwemikong. Since that time he has lived up to the spirit of Bebaminojmat, "one who goes around talking in a good way." (Also translated as "one who talks honestly in an open way of truth.) Later, he approached his mother to find out that he is part of the Loon Clan, according to his father's lineage.

"Nice," he smiled. "I like the loon."

Because he has made it a priority, Anishinaabe culture and history provide a foundation for his life, his music and his art.

"I experienced a defining moment at Dreamer's Rock. And it inspired me to start working and to discover everything I could about Anishinaabe civilization. I am continuing to research my Anishinaabe heritage. All the paradigms are there; I just have to tap into it. You could never run out of ideas," he stressed. "Because of the concentric nature of Anishinaabe knowledge, you are continually discovering and learning. And a lot of Anishinaabe knowledge is generated right here on Manitoulin Island."

As he developed his style, he simultaneously studied shamanism. As a member of the Three Fires Midewiwin Society, he has worked to integrate his spirituality and his art.

Looking back, he recognized that the 1970s were years of consciousness raising and confidence building.

"There were a lot of brave Indians at that time," he said. "They stood up at a time when many in society looked down upon Native people. Later, people began to identify themselves tribally and soon people began to identify themselves as Anishinaabe."

Whenever he shares his journey with others, he reinforces the liberating nature of Anishinaabe knowledge and practices. His commitment has become a powerful force for good in the lives of First Nations youth.

In his creative process, Leland has avoided scattering his energies. Instead, he has generally opted to concentrate on a particular principle or element and explore the chosen idea at ever deeper levels. The values of simplicity, duality, balance and fluidity have always characterized his work. Predictably, consistency has emerged as one of his strongest assets. In future, he hopes to help other seekers by publishing his views on the concentric nature of existence.

Meanwhile, he has become firmly established in the firmament of revered First Nations artists. Examples of his commissioned work can be viewed at the Anishinaabe Spiritual Centre at Anderson Lake near Espanola, the Birch Island band office on the Whitefish River First Nation and the Canadian Native Arts Foundation in Toronto. In addition, he has created posters for "Artists Against Racism," in Toronto, the "Festival of Thanksgiving," in M'Chigeeng, "Heritage Canada," in Ottawa and "Health Careers Canada."

He originated logos for a wide variety of organizations as well. Whitefish Lake First Nation, "Family Violence Prevention," Neechi Institute, "Addiction Awareness," Shkagamik-Kwe Health Centre, "Women's Health" and the Wikwemikong Community Living Association, all proudly display his logo designs. A 9' x 40' mural painted at Laurentian University and another 10' x 10' mural at Trent University, provide further evidence of his versatility.

The Ojibwe Cultural Foundation used his talents to produce educational materials on the Seven Teachings. And he has even designed a T-shirt for Amnesty International. Book and magazine covers also display his unique illustrations.

Solo exhibitions include the Northern Craft Gallery, South Bay Mouth (1984), The Wahsa Gallery, Winnipeg (1982), the First Man Gallery, Calgary (1980), and the Walter Engel Gallery, Toronto (1979).

Leland has also participated in many group exhibitions. For instance, he contributed to the Whetung Art Gallery show (1999), the Buckhorn Art Festival and the Children of the Raven Gallery (1997), the Edmonton Convention Centre and Laurentian Museum and Arts Centre (1984). Prior to that he took part in the Tundra Art Gallery show (1982), the Anishnaabe Mee-kun Travelling Art Exhibition (1981), and Dr. Bernard Cinader's juried exhibition in Switzerland (1980).

His work also received widespread attention during a travelling exhibit entitled, "The Manitou Collection: Celebrating the Spirit of the People". The touring show of 38 thematically related works by nine Anishinaabe artists was organized by the WKP Kennedy Public Art Gallery and the Manitou Conference of the United Church of Canada. The exhibition of paintings, prints and drawings, held by the church since 1988, also featured Don Assinewai, Mel Madahbee, James Jocko, Doug Fox, Stanley Panamick, Blair Debassige, Randy Trudeau and Tim Trudeau.

The collection was on display in M'Chigeeng, Thunder Bay, Sault Ste. Marie, Haileybury, North Bay, Brantford, Timmins and Sudbury. The event marked the 20th anniversary of the United Church of Canada's first official apology to First Nations peoples. The tour was intended as a catalyst for building respect and understanding among cultures.

In the acrylic canvases of the early 1980s, viewers can see evidence of his strong grounding in the narrative tradition of the Anishinaabe. His paintings depict the offering of tobacco, the gift of the sacred colours, the medicine wheel, the search for the sacred scroll and a prayer to the four winds. Other works celebrate family ties and the intimate connection to Mother Earth. He has gone on to elaborate on many of these themes over the course of his career.

Along the way, he has maintained his love of music and song writing. He was proud to record *Mishomis*, which was included in a Juno award winning compilation CD.

Institutions such as Laurentian University, in Sudbury, have paid tribute to his talent and his humanitarian work. In June 2008, Leland was presented with an honourary Doctorate of Letters during convocation ceremonies.

"Highly respected and regarded in our community, Leland is well-known for advocating values of respect, harmony, kindness and tolerance. As well, he has an innate ability to look for the good in people and in situations," said Sheila Cote-Meek, director, academic for Native Affairs. She praised him for his willingness to respond to community needs and his "uncanny ability to make people laugh."

Leland is often called upon to address academic audiences and to discuss the role of First Nations art in the Canadian art scene. But he grows impatient with the recurring debate, the never ending questions raised about the relevance of Native art. In his view, Anishinaabe artists don't need places such as the National Gallery of Canada or the Museum of Man to endorse their value.

"We come from a long line of creativity; our civilization goes way back. What we practise is creativity; it's in our tradition. We don't need those places because there is such a surge of creativity coming from our communities," he emphasized.

In public presentations, he continues to express admiration for beadwork, birch-bark crafts and other creative endeavours in his home community. "That's where I come from; that's the body of knowledge that I carry on my back. I am proud to carry that tradition."

If he is asked, why Canadian society is finally beginning to accept Native art, he has been quick to respond. "I think it is because they are just growing up."

If he had his way, Manitoulin's Native artists would join forces to establish an Anishinaabe research institute. He has been urging other artists to assist in the mission to further refine what it means to be Anishinaabe. Undoubtedly, First Nations have been affected by mainstream assimilation tactics and by modern technology, but he believes many cultural tenets are timeless.

"We are dealing with a different Anishinaabe people now. We are not the same people we were a hundred years ago and we are not the same people we were in the 1960s, but we are still Anishinaabe people," he said.

Travelling and interacting with people from different nations, has helped Leland reinforce his goals and his vision over the past three decades. For him Anishinaabe culture serves as the foundation of his strength and courage.

Although he has maintained a residence in Sudbury, Leland has been returning to his Manitoulin roots each summer. His studio/gallery on Eshkibok Road in Wikwemikong has been welcoming a steady stream of visitors. Although he enjoys the socializing, he still makes it a priority to set time aside for his own meditation and painting.

"Solitude is very important part of my life; when I paint it is in solitude. I get all my instruments ready and then it's time to get in the zone," he said.

After a lifetime of dialectical thinking he has trained himself to think in Anishinaabe form, line and composition. For him, the study of history and the human condition is ongoing. "I have enjoyed my life as a visual artist. I will continue to challenge myself and to get out of my comfort zone."

He remains optimistic about the future of Aboriginal art as the population of First Nations grows. And he foresees a powerful group of artists emerging.

"We see a surge in numbers as well as a surge in creativity in our communities. I bet there will be Anishinaabe art that is so strong that there won't be any questions about who we are," he predicted.

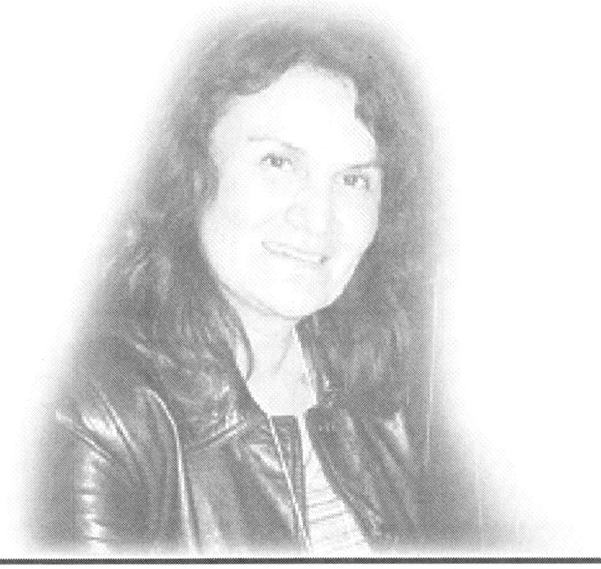

CHAPTER 3

DR. SHIRLEY CHEECHOO (1952 -): Healing Through Storytelling

Like most children, Shirley Cheechoo enjoyed an active fantasy life when she was growing up. From an early age, her imagination knew no bounds; she felt a strong desire to act, to tell stories and to express herself creatively.

Today she is an internationally recognized trail-blazer and visual artist. She came to prominence as a playwright in 1992, with the production of *Path With No Moccasins*. Later she paved the way for other First Nations artists when she became the first Native person to write, produce, direct and act in a dramatic feature length film in Canada. Her production entitled, *Bearwalker*, was screened at the Sundance Film Festival in 2000.

But, despite the accolades, it has not been an easy road to success for the sensitive girl born in Eastmain, Quebec in 1952, and raised in Northern Ontario. Along the way she has encountered both gender and racial discrimination.

Although film projects often take her to sets across the globe, she always retreats to her home on Manitoulin Island to recuperate and reconnect with her family. Ensconced in the familiar surroundings of Kasheese Studios, in M'Chigeeng, she has found the solitude necessary for planning her next venture.

Although her busy schedule leaves little time for distractions, she can sometimes be persuaded to reflect on her formative years and to articulate the goals she has set for the coming years.

Acting seemed to come naturally when she was a child living near Hearst, Ontario. Over the years she has often paid tribute to her parents and grandparents for encouraging her innate yearning to tell stories. Her mother, in particular, taught her to rely on her dreams for guidance.

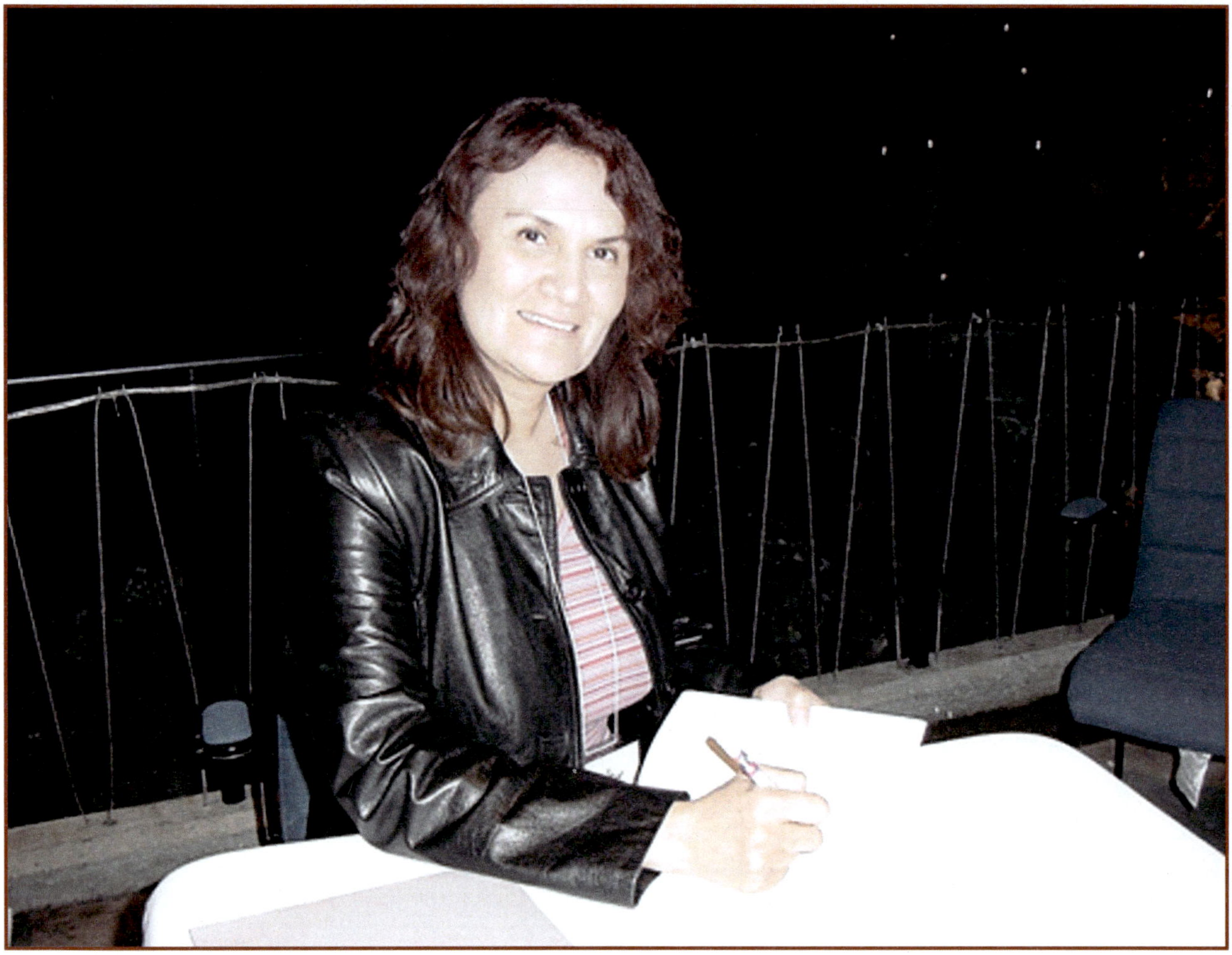

“My mother was a writer, but I never realized that until she passed away,” Ms. Cheechoo said. “She was a great story teller.”

In fact, the whole family had a flair for the dramatic. Her father would amuse the children by playacting the antics of an animal and challenging the youngsters to guess what kind of creature he was mimicking.

“They were just games to us then,” she said. “However, the seeds of acting and storytelling were already planted and modelled for us.”

Life in remote Moose Factory and Hearst often required people to invent their own entertainment.

“My brother, Roger, and I would do skits for the community,” she recalled. “It was just for fun. And we used to see movies at the local hall so that inspired us to create our own skits.”

Even the oppressive atmosphere of the residential schools in Ontario could not stifle her natural curiosity and imagination. She immersed herself in Elvis movies, Zorro adventures and Hollywood westerns on Saturdays. Little did her teachers know that one day those experiences would be fodder for powerful plays and films.

As a teenager, Shirley discovered an outlet for her talents during a series of art camps held at Schreiber Island in Lake Huron. Tom Peltier, of Wikwemikong, had organized the workshops and had invited Native youth from throughout the province to participate in the unique gathering. Under the tutelage of such luminaries as Daphne Odjig, Carl Ray and Duke Redbird, the timid youngsters had a chance to gain confidence.

"I sampled everything that was there; music, drama, art, film," she said. "Anything we wanted to experience was available to us. We had mentors, of course, but it was all left to us to imagine and to bring it alive."

She smiled at the memory of how shy the workshop participants were in those days. To make them feel more comfortable expressing themselves, Duke Redbird suggested they try "shadow theatre." That method worked so well that eventually they were able to take the curtain away and step into the spotlight.

In the decades to follow, she would find herself increasingly in the limelight as she found she excelled in many different pursuits. In April 1984, she tried her hand at modelling and took New York by storm after only five weeks of training at the Gauvreau School of Fine Arts, in Sudbury. She participated in an event to mark the 25th anniversary of the World Modelling Association of America. Her first advent on to the catwalk netted her the top Canadian Model title. In the competition, she wore clothing designed by Sheshegwaning's Deborah Pitawanakwat.

Shirley formed Spokensong Productions in 1997, and premiered *Silent Tears*, at the Sundance Film Festival in 1998, where she won the "Telefilm Canada" award for Best Canadian Aboriginal Language Television Program. Among her many documentary credits are, *Tracks in the Snow* and *Dancing River*. The films were commissioned by the Cree School Board of James Bay and produced in Cree and English to help students learn more about their culture.

The generosity of her early role models moved her to recreate similar opportunities for other First Nations youth. She founded De-ba-jeh-mu-jig Theatre Company, an organization that continues to thrive as an integral part of Manitoulin summer attractions.

"Tom (Peltier) gave me the opportunity to experience these things and since I am the next generation, I want to work with youth and allow them to explore the arts as well. The arts really helped me to come out of my shell and helped me to heal from my residential school experiences. The arts are a very powerful medium for healing and I want to help youth to experience things they may never have had the opportunity to experience."

With these goals in mind, Shirley has established Weengushk film institute on Manitoulin Island, to nurture First Nations expertise in cinema. Although it took persistence and patience, her hard work finally paid off in 2008. Agencies such as the Ontario

Trillium Foundation and FedNor provided some initial funding support. And, as reported in the Manitoulin Expositor (September 24, 2008), CTV GlobeMedia presented a cheque for $35,000, to Weengushk, for administration and marketing purposes. The ceremony took place in Sudbury during the Cinefest Film Festival.

"It's really overwhelming," Shirley told the Expositor. "Just knowing that there's people out there that actually believe in the same dream that I have. I'm hoping that this will create some kind of chain where other people will learn about our film institute and be able to support it in the same kind of way."

From her experiences with youth on the sets of previous films, she has observed their keen interest in finding work in the business.

"We will be training artists to find themselves, to share their stories and to learn all aspects of film making," she noted. "It's time for us to be able to tell our own stories. Those are learned from our elders, and our language, and our culture, and to be able to show people that this is coming from us, this is our voice. We need to do that. Once we develop that voice, I think the film industry in Northern Ontario will increase."

Shirley learned the ropes herself through sheer determination and an unwavering resolve to break down barriers. Her business savvy grew as her work was screened at Sundance Film Festival, the ImaginNative Film Festival, Montreal's First People's Festival, the Santa Fe Film Festival and the American Indian Film Festival of San Francisco. In 2002 she was named, "Independent Film-maker of the Year," at the Arizona International Film Institute.

Shirley credits Robert Redford and the Sundance Institute for providing valuable professional development opportunities for emerging screenwriters and directors such as herself.

Being accepted into the Canadian Film Centre, established by renowned Canadian director Norman Jewison, was also an encouraging milestone. It was an important step forward in her mission to dispel stereotypes of the original peoples perpetuated in Hollywood movies.

"I am the first Aboriginal director to be accepted," she reported in an "Ontario Birchbark interview" in May 2002. "I tried once before, but it didn't happen. Then suddenly the program director called and now I will be living in Toronto. It is a great opportunity and a great honour to get in. It will open a lot of doors for us as First Nations film-makers. It will give us a chance to share our culture and to educate the producers, actors, directors and other professionals in the field about the way we live as people."

Eventually, numerous plum assignments came her way. In August 2006, Ms. Cheechoo embarked on an eight month directing journey that took her and her crew to ten countries. They filmed in remote villages in the Arctic Circle, Europe, Africa and South America. The mission involved examining the herbal remedies used by indigenous healers, shamans and medicine people in a variety of cultures from Ireland and Wales to

Peru and Guatemala. Cameras followed the explorations of Dr. Daniele Behn Smith, a 27 year old Eh-Cho Dene doctor from British Columbia.

Medicine Woman, the series created from this quest, has been shown on Vision TV, APTN and SCN. The project was created by Norm Wilkinson of Australia's Visionquest Entertainment and co-produced with Gerry Sperling of 4 Square Productions.

Now a veteran in the film industry, Shirley has become accustomed to being on the road.

"I do a lot of travel for my work," she said. "Travel really opens up your imagination; it opens up your heart. Often you realize how lucky you are. Sometimes I like to share what I have with other cultures and I try to learn from them as well."

The intensity of this cross-continental project has had a lasting impact on her world view. Nestled in her comfortable home on Manitoulin, she has found her thoughts continually returning to those far away places.

"When I go back in memory, I think about the people of Africa, the people of Peru and Guatemala and Sri Lanka. When I sit here I often think about them," she confided. "I would like to touch them again and I'd like to visit there again."

One bond in particular tugs at her heart strings. She was befriended by the wife of a chief of the San Bushmen, one of the oldest inhabitants of southern Africa.

"I have an adopted grandmother in Africa," she revealed. "Before I left she gave me an African name; she called me 'sweetheart,' a name that is very important to the people there. Here the word is such a throwaway thing, but there it is very meaningful."

Excursions to diverse parts of the planet have reinforced her belief in the healing power of storytelling.

"When you tell true stories, you tap into people's hearts, you tap into people's spirits," she said. "And if they have had similar experiences, they may heal themselves. It doesn't matter how old you are or what race you are; it's all universal."

The shy youngster who attended the Shreiber Island art camps so long ago, has won national and international acclaim in recent years. On March 7, 2007, she accepted a prestigious "National Aboriginal Achievement Award" at a Toronto ceremony. For her the recognition was extra special. "It's coming from the Aboriginal community and it helps you move forward as an artist, because you know you have support," she said.

On June 26, 2008 Shirley enjoyed another peak experience when she received a lifetime achievement award at the Talking Stick Film Festival in Santa Fe, New Mexico. During the festival she was praised for her accomplishments as an actor, writer, producer, playwright and visual artist and honoured for her contributions to Aboriginal filmmaking. Viewers had an opportunity to see several of her films including *Medicine River, Bearwalker, Pikutiskwauu* and *Johnny Tootall.*

Although developing new film projects and establishing new facilities posed many challenges, Shirley has always offered encouraging words for the students following in her path. She believes it is her gift and responsibility to pass knowledge down from one generation to the next.

"If you have a dream, don't let anyone tell you that you can't do it, don't let anyone stop you from doing it," she advised. "It's important to have a dream, because sooner or later it will come true. If it doesn't come true in your life time, someone younger will follow your path and make it happen. Just keep on knocking on doors and they'll eventually open."

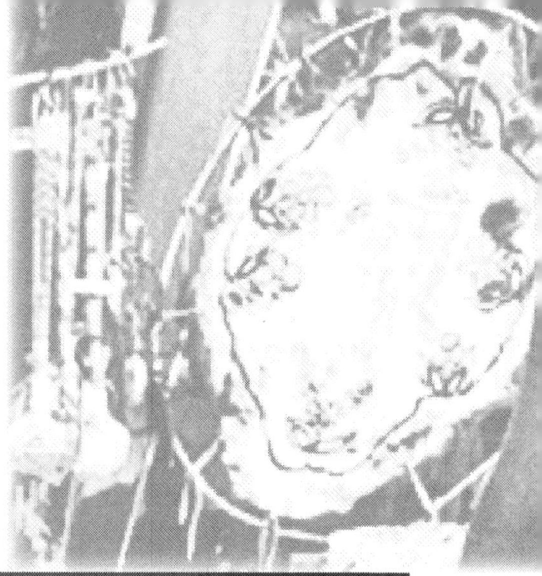

MICHAEL CYWINK (1955 -): Searching for meaning in a topsy turvy world

CHAPTER 4

The search for identity and a sense of purpose in life is an age-old quest. It is simply a part of the human condition to seek answers to the ultimate questions: where did I come from? Why have I been placed on Earth? What is the best way to use my gifts and talents?

Like other truth-seekers before him, artist Michael Cywink has pondered and weighed these perplexing matters. His reflections are revealed in a twenty-five page perfect-bound book published by Rain Books Inc. *The Adventures of Crazy Turtle* appeals to readers of all ages.

The Canadian publishing establishment remains a difficult realm for First Nations authors to penetrate, he noted during his book launch. It took several attempts to find a publisher for the colourful adventure. And it required some perseverance before Burlington-based Rain Publishing expressed an interest in promoting the title as a children's story.

Although the act of writing doesn't come to him as smoothly as the act of adding paint to canvas, he felt a need to get the story expressed after many years of wrestling with the vision.

"Writing a book is a long awaited goal," he said. "Everyone must have a creation story that allows him or her to express their individual gift, which in itself is their life. Crazy Turtle is not me, but a piece of all of us. There is no end to a creation story so there is no end to the adventures of Crazy Turtle."

He believes many readers will identify with the struggles of the main character as he is caught in a maelstrom of turmoil he doesn't quite understand. When the world seems to be coming down around your ears, the first instinct is to protect yourself, the tale suggests.

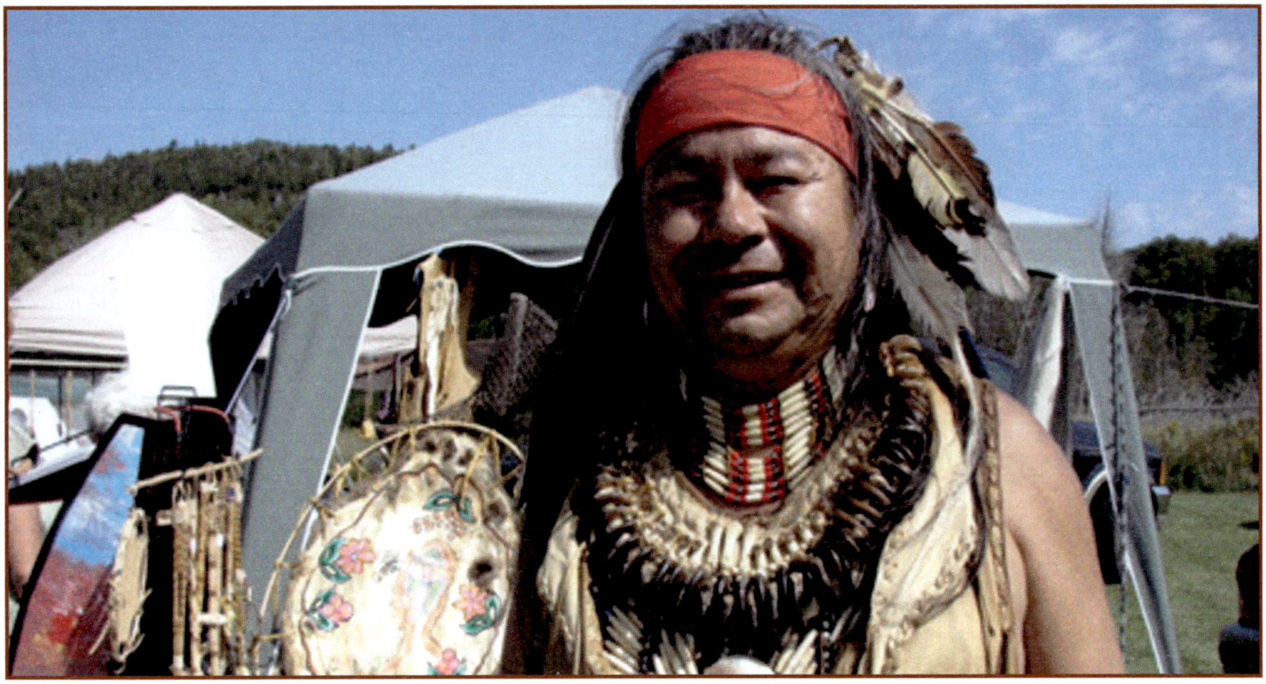

"We hide inside our shells; we hide inside our thoughts and feelings. And we build invisible walls around us to hide and protect our being, our true feelings," Michael said. "But Crazy Turtle goes beyond that. Crazy Turtle brings out a truth in us that we need no longer hide; we need no longer go away and try to run from our inner being."

In his view, it is important to remember that humans are spirit beings living in the physical gift of creation and that we are not human beings looking for a spirit.

"This is a story for all ages," he reiterated. "It is meant to help one understand the spirit being inside their shell."

According to an excerpt from the book, the turtle imagery has been present in the back of Michael's mind since his teen years. The original seeds of the creation story first emerged in the 1970s. As an impressionable youth, he was drawn to listen to his community Elders swapping local legends. These tales "would send chills through you," he recalled. But it wasn't until after he had travelled many miles and encountered many different cultures that he felt compelled to share the teachings. In 2006, this phase of the odyssey emerged in print accompanied by vibrant illustrations. The official launch of the publication took place at the Canadian Aboriginal Festival, in Toronto.

The fusion of cross-cultural knowledge present in his artwork and writing came together after intense personal exploration. Curiosity, and perhaps restlessness, spurred him to hitchhike across Turtle Island (North America). In his travels, he often sought to unravel some of the mysteries of life in both a universal and a personal context.

Michael, also known as Miizhen, traces his origins to Whitefish Falls, an area steeped in legend and Anishinaabe tradition. He is currently a registered band member with the Wikwemikong Unceded Indian Reserve. In his youth, he left the familiar territory of Dreamer's Rock to study commercial and graphic design at George Brown College and Sault College. Enrolment in the museum studies program at the Institute of American Indian Arts in Santa Fe, New Mexico gave him an opportunity to expand his horizons. In addition, an internship as a First Nations consultant with Walt Disney Imagineering in Glendale, California, added to his knowledge of creation myths. And, finally, a stint as curator at the Ojibwe Cultural Foundation (OCF) on Manitoulin Island also served to enrich his aesthetic and spiritual values.

The OCF, first established in 1974 to preserve and enhance Ojibwe language and culture, has been a steadfast supporter of Anishinaabe artists. As curator, Michael collaborated with other arts organizations and continued the OCF's mission to showcase and nurture up-and-coming Native artists. He was pleased to play a key role in a landmark symposium featuring prominent Native and non-Native artists held in M'Chigeeng First Nation in July 2004.

He remains an active member of the Aboriginal Curatorial Collective and the Canadian Aboriginal Arts Administrators group.

Throughout his own artistic development, Michael has been a conscientious practitioner of what he describes as "the indigenous creative process." Everything from the story conception through to the illustrative process is directly from the artist, he emphasized.

His personal art portfolio mirrors his inventiveness with intricate mobiles, murals and photo collages. Visitors to his online gallery will see mixed media creations such as stretched deer hide painted with acrylics and decorated with feathers, deer bone, shell or horsehair.

He continues to experiment with various symbolic interpretations as he strives for versatility and authenticity.

"Art in all its hidden conceptions seems to me as a vehicle used to transport ideas beyond mere sight," he said. "Art in itself contains all viable possibilities in expressions."

In the introduction to Crazy Turtle's journey, Michael described some unforgettable and damaging encounters he had with mainstream educational and religious institutions. And he revealed the transforming power of a vision quest he experienced as a youngster. He remembered an interlude of soul travel as he surrendered to the sensation of soaring beyond this mortal plane yet retaining conscious connection.

In the beginning of the adventure, he related how an "unusual" summer stirred up the taste of sulphur and evoked images of hot springs and "a volcano spewing." As the story unfolds, the reader is encouraged to leave the rational, mundane existence behind and to accompany the author to another dimension.

Although the reader is transported on a roller coaster ride of spinning, tumbling and falling, the journey is ultimately a healing experience.

"I do consider the book therapeutic," he confirmed. "It has certainly done wonders for me from my end of things. I know this adventure of Crazy Turtle just doesn't stop. It's a story that never ends."

Employing art for self-discovery and inspirational purposes has long been a passion for Michael. In several past projects, he has utilized art in a therapeutic manner with children, youth and adults.

"Art, whether it is in writing, painting or carving is for me therapy for my living spirit," he added. "Art is a gift of historical recovery."

Michael hopes his readers can take a lesson from the saga of Crazy Turtle. We can stop hiding in our shells; we can emerge to freely explore and celebrate beauty both inside and out.

In 2008, he followed some of his own sage advice and took advantage of an opportunity to collaborate with an international gathering of artists. As a result, a formerly unadorned wall in the thriving town of Holguin, Cuba now displays the distinctive outline of Manitoulin Island surrounded by First Nations clan symbols and floral motifs. The 27 by 15 foot mural stands as vibrant testimony to the artistic revolution taking place on this once isolated island nation.

The creation of the colourful mural in Holguin (pop. 300,000) was all part of the 15th annual "Romerias de Mayo Festival," an event that draws over a thousand young intellectuals and artists from all continents plus all the Cuban provinces to a marathon week of cultural exchange. This festival, which ran May 2-8, served as a preamble to the World Young Artists Festival, slated for 2009.

The Romerias de Mayo concept, came into being in 1993, when a group of young artists decided to organize a venue to share their diverse artistic endeavours. Since then it has evolved into an intense week of activities involving musicians, artists, dancers, writers, actors and researchers. Workshops start early each morning and delegates take part in conferences, symposiums, expositions and stage shows until well into the night.

The gathering captured the imagination of Michael when he received an invitation from Alexis Triana Hernandez, president of the organizing committee. "We summon artists from all over the planet to be here for our World Festival of Artistic Youths," he wrote. "We believe your work will suit the purposes of the festival. You represent a culture almost extinct among us; only a few aboriginal descendants remain despite what has been done to preserve their culture, which has several features common to your own aboriginal origins. By working with those descendants, the people of Cuba and the artists from other countries participating in the event, we will defend our common aboriginal culture."

The rugged mountainous region known as Holguin, is famous for a park and statues commemorating the arrival of Christopher Columbus in 1492. When the Europeans explored this island it was part of the Great Maniabon Indian territory. Historical plaques erected at Holguin commemorate the fateful meeting of European and Aboriginal civilizations.

It was a challenge Michael could not ignore. He has made it his mission to relate the history of the First Peoples wherever he travels. So when he was also urged to speak at the Our Memory (Memoria Nuestra) theoretical event as well, he determined he would "speak on my experiences defending my culture and passing this cultural knowledge on to the new generations." He started approaching sponsors for the once in a lifetime adventure in Cuba and before long he had the support of the Wikwemikong Heritage Organization, and the Canada Council of the Arts. The festival organizing committee covered all the lodging, food and transportation costs once he arrived in Holguin.

Since the first few days of the festival are devoted to tradition, Michael decided to design a wall mural featuring woodland floral images and dodems (spirit helpers), which would be representative of the Anishinaabe of the Great Lakes. It was his sincere wish that "this cultural sharing may help bring the history of the Anishinaabe into a clearer international vision and help unify the vision of the indigenous people partaking in this event."

Needless to say, he had his work cut out for him as a cultural ambassador. Some of the Cuban people perceived him as somewhat of an exotic visitor with his long hair, eagle feathers, bear claw and deer hide accessories.

"The Cuban perception of Canada is that it's all ice and snow. Many thought that I was an Eskimo; they thought I came from Alaska or the North Pole. They had never had an Eskimo down in Cuba before," he laughed.

Naturally, the "Canadian Eskimo" was regarded as a celebrity and attracted a great deal of media attention. He was featured on Cuban national television several times, he reported. But once the mural project started to take shape, there were many opportunities to dispel stereotypes and educate viewers about Anishinaabe heritage.

"I helped them overcome many misconceptions," he said. "I showed them some traditional art such as breast plates and deer hide. I told them the history of the Ottawa people and I talked about pre-contact before the Europeans came to Turtle Island."

Throughout the exchange, he worked with Juan Carlos Anzardo and Nalia Martines Grau, two senior master muralists plus Ibrahim Ambar Richardo and Yail Parras Guerra, two students from the local art academy. To facilitate communication, interpreters Aniely Fernandez Torres and Maikel Ballester Gutierrez assisted Michael in guiding the brushstrokes of his apprentices.

"First they put a layer of ochre on the wall and then they applied blues and reds over top," he explained. Slowly an archetypal Woodland scene emerged with the shape of Manitoulin Island, the resting place of the Creator, drawn in the centre surrounded by flowers and strawberries. The outline of the island melts into an iconic representation of the Great Lakes water spirit. A wolf serving as protector and teacher, peers out from a backdrop of towering evergreen trees. Nearby, a majestic deer stands as the symbol of understanding and compassion. It is accompanied by the moose, long associated with strength and endurance. The two kings of the forest survey their domain amidst a knot of cat-tails. Hand prints placed on the wall earlier are transformed into bear paw prints to signify leadership.

"My interest in designing the mural was to leave a part of our nation with the descendants of the original people of Cuba," he said. "It was a gift from the Anishinaabe nations of Manitoulin, the island of the spirits, to the community of Holguin, Cuba. Through our colour, we put our healing energies into the wall to share with all who see it. They in turn will share the medicine of healing so that they too can feel its energy in a good way."

Since the mural project was a new addition to the festival program, he felt it was important for both the artists and the viewers to feel uplifted by the project.

"This was the first time a mural was completed at the event," he noted. "It took us three days. It was quite a challenge, but we had interpreters to help me convey the stories and the spiritual interpretations of the symbols. We had to work in stifling heat so a lot of the work was done in the evening when it was cooler."

Before his departure for home, Michael presented copies of his publication *The Adventures of Crazy Turtle* to Alexis Triana Hernandez, the provincial director of culture of Holguin and to Abel Prieto, the national minister of culture. And since it is traditional for participants to present a flag and a soil sample to their hosts, he gave his Cuban counterparts a Canadian flag with Manitoulin superimposed over the maple leaf.

"I was not representing Canada," he explained. "I was representing the Anishinaabe of the Great Lakes and Manitoulin."

The Canadian delegation to Holguin was the largest group at this year's festival. A contingent of artists from Concordia University in Montreal was especially well-received, he said. He speculates that Cuba still has strong bonds with Quebec because former prime minister Pierre Elliot Trudeau was a staunch ally of Cuban president Fidel Castro.

As he reflected on his time in Cuba, Michael was eager to return for additional collaboration in the future. He envisioned taking some young artists from the Manitoulin area with him. For him there is much potential for an "island to island" exchange involving theatre, art, research and writing.

"There's a lot of respect for Canadians in Cuba," he said. "It was a real eye-opener for me and I want other artists to see just how amazing it is to leave Manitoulin and journey to the salt water island they call Cuba."

In his view, "There is a revolution going on in Cuba and it's with the arts."

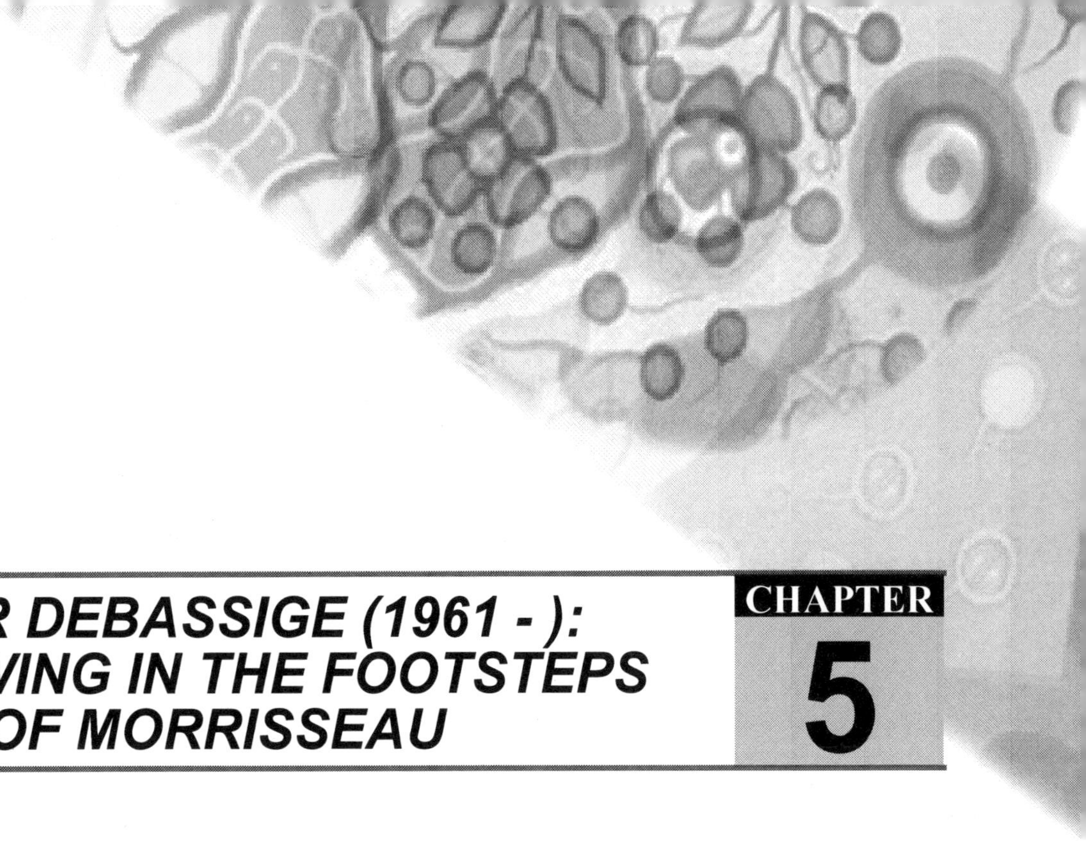

CHAPTER 5

BLAIR DEBASSIGE (1961 -): FOLLOWING IN THE FOOTSTEPS OF MORRISSEAU

Norval Morrisseau, the founder of the Woodland School of Art, passed away in December 2007 at the age of 75. The man known as "The Picasso of the North" undoubtedly influenced his own generation as well as a succession of young Native artists who followed his lead over the past four decades.

Born on Sand Point reserve near Beardmore on March 14, 1932, Morrisseau was the oldest of seven boys. He was raised by his maternal grandparents and immersed in the legends and ceremonies of his people.

In 1962, a momentous encounter with Toronto artist and curator, Jackson Pollock, led to widespread exposure in the mainstream Canadian art community. When he published *Legends of my People, the Great Ojibway* in 1965, his reputation grew. As art critics look back over his career, most credit him with founding an innovative school of art, although it took 44 years for him to get a solo exhibition at Canada's national gallery.

The Woodland School, as it is known, was inspired by his grandfather's teachings and imagery from ancient birchbark scrolls and rock paintings. Woodland painting was also dubbed, "medicine painting," because Morrisseau introduced new artistic conventions to convey spiritual themes. For example, he created x-ray anatomy with spirit lines radiating from the spines of animals and spirit creatures. Through this x-ray style, he attempted to reveal the souls of his subjects and in the process to enhance cross-cultural understanding.

As curator Greg Hill explained in the catalogue accompanying Morrisseau's 2006 Ottawa exhibit, "The interiors of living things are shown with a stylized skeletal structure often embellished by linear design elements and sometimes incorporating an interior animal or spirit being." According to Hill, Morrisseau was a "shaman artist" who transformed visions into tangible forms of expression. And, in the process, he created controversy because many First Nations people believed it was a sacrilege to reveal the sacred ways to non-Natives.

Although he will be remembered and revered as a master colourist and inventor of unique visual language, Morrisseau had a difficult life journey. He experienced a myriad of physical, emotional and spiritual setbacks. In childhood he survived residential school abuse; as a teenager he battled tuberculosis and as an adult he suffered severe burns in a hotel fire. Alcohol proved to be an impediment to his career on many occasions. And then in his 70s, he was diagnosed with Parkinson's disease.

Although he faced some-times overwhelming obstacles, Morrisseau achieved many remarkable milestones. In 1967, he created memorable murals at Expo 67, in Montreal and in 1973, he was appointed to the Royal Academy of Art."The Order of Canada" was bestowed upon him in 1978. Honourary degrees were presented to him by McMaster University in 1980 and the Laurentian University in 2007. France honoured him during their bicentennial of the French Revolution in 1989. He accepted an eagle feather from the Assembly of First Nations in 1995. Eventually, a long overdue tribute came in 2006 when he became the first Aboriginal artist to mount a solo exhibition at the National Gallery of Canada. This hard-won recognition paved the way for Daphne Odjig's retrospective in 2008 and Carl Beam's show slated for 2010.

As the Father of the Wood-land School, Morrisseau has served as a universal role model. Many First Nations artists started by adopt-ing his subject matter and conventions before moving on to develop their own personal styles.

Manitoulin Island artist, Blair Debassige, is just one example of a present day practitioner devoted to preserving the Morrisseau legacy. He is proud to paint in the Woodland style and to follow in the footsteps of his mentor.

Blair, owner of the Nimkee Gallery in M'Chigeeng First Nation, spent his childhood in the idyllic natural setting of Manitoulin and started painting at age nine. A self-described "day dreamer," he was drawn to spend many solo hours in the forest near his home. He describes human beings are "enviro-organisms," attuned to the energy and the Great Mystery of the natural world.

As for his life's vocation, Blair believes that the call to create is deeply embedded in an individual's DNA code. In his view, some people are born to be teachers, others to be construction workers or even lumberjacks. People will always find their niche. For him, the impulse to be an artist was always there.

"I knew when I was a kid that I was different, that I was a loner," he confided. "I always liked to be in the woods. I found there was a comfort there because the trees have energy."

As he grew older, he tried his hand at painting on a variety of objects, including shields, drums and breast-plates. He has been exhibiting his oils, acrylics, birchbark and rawhide work since 1977.

The "Manitou Collection" showcased Blair's bold colours and evocative symbolism in 2006. The touring exhibition visited M'Chigeeng, Thunder Bay, Sault Ste. Marie, Haileybury, North Bay, Timmins, Sudbury and Brantford. The show was held in conjunction with the 20th anniversary of the United Church of Canada's first official apology to First Nations Peoples.

Of all his accomplishments, Blair is especially proud of a fringed deer hide stole he created for Pope John Paul to wear at World Youth Day in Toronto in 2002. The opportunity to craft the gift came during a time of personal struggle, he related. Although he had been maintaining sobriety and trying to follow the Red Path, it had been a constant challenge. Then one momentous evening, a period of solitude and reflection led him to the answer.

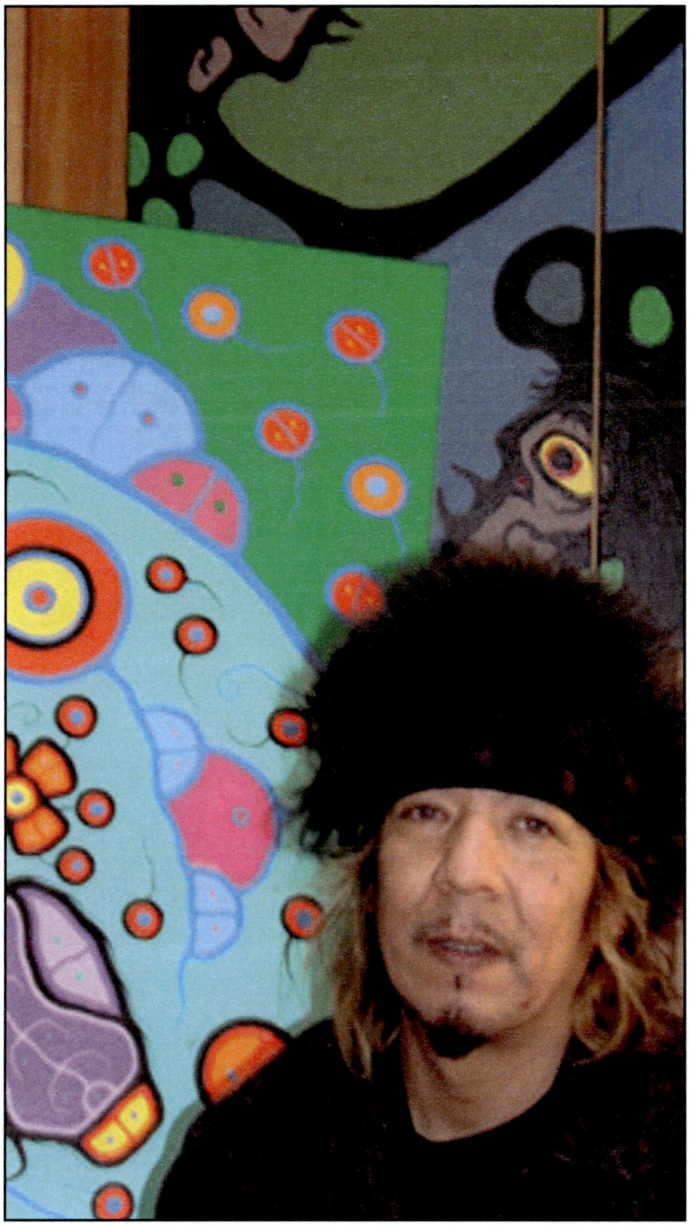

"I was surrounded by a feeling of unconditional love," he said. "I didn't want it to leave. When I woke up the next morning, there was something different about me that I couldn't quite put my finger on."

He reached out to Catholic Church officials who encouraged him to heed the vision and to use his gifts in meaningful ways. Soon he found himself freed of his desire to drink and called to express a higher purpose through his artwork. He was sent a simple deer hide stole to decorate for Pope John Paul's appearance in July. When completed, the garment was a testimony to the Anishinaabe philosophy of living in harmony with nature. It displayed Blair's love of traditional Ojibway bird, animal and flower motifs.

"I chose to include birds, they are the messengers, they are in the songs, the language, and in the stories; they connect us back to nature," he explained.

The presentation of the Papal stole was just one small step in his spiritual quest. Blair's soul-searching had been accelerated when Norval Morrisseau visited M'Chigeeng in the 1990s. At that time, Morrisseau was in ill health but still articulate and willing to share his vision. Blair forged a bond with the shaman artist that remains strong long after the death of his mentor.

"The last time that I met him in person was in 1995,"Blair recalled. "He said that he was sorry he couldn't be with me in person when I was going through a rough time. Later we continued to talk on the phone about four times a week before the Parkinson's disease and the emphysema made it too difficult for him."

Although they were separated by thousands of miles, the two artists communicated in a unique way. They traded works of art and Morrisseau would instruct Blair to gather certain medicines for him and to send them to British Columbia. Blair also collected birch bark for the scrolls Morrisseau painted. In turn, the Elder gave Blair his pipes, eagle feathers and bear claws as well as spiritual guidance.

"Norval said to be bold and daring in your work and in life," he said. "Paint, paint, paint and take chances; even when you are going through troubles, keep on painting."

Through Morrisseau's teachings, Blair came to identify with the concept of tribal memory or the "collective imagination" as a source for art. As years pass, language and tradition disintegrate, he said, so it is important to pay attention to the images that come from memories.

"When I went through a period of self-discovery, I asked myself why I was painting legends," Blair said. "When I get a deja vu feeling when I am working on a painting, it is because our people go back thousands of years. I am carrying an emotion that a Native person had five thousand years ago. I am carrying fragments of that in my DNA and I am preserving a lot of that when I paint. Our culture is rich and we don't want the culture to be lost."

Talks with the Woodland Elder had also encouraged Blair to investigate the "science of colour" and to avoid the dull, muted colours that characterized European paintings. Since Morrisseau's work has always been praised for its vibrancy and its hypnotic effect on the viewer, Blair strives for a similar 3-D effect.

"Colour can evoke many emotions," he stated. "Norval told me to use bright colours and to paint how I feel inside. Images can pull you in or call to you. Some colours can evoke your Native ancestry."

Blair was also impressed by Morrisseau's view that art can play a role in healing humans in some aspects of their lives. As he grappled with his own demons, Blair found solace in the Elder's philosophy. And he particularly enjoyed the fact that they both belong to the Bear Clan. He continued to pick his own medicines, to participate in the sweat lodge and to study the language and culture of his people.

"Sometimes compulsion and craving gets in the way," Blair acknowledged. "But I got to a better place through my art. I thank Norval for what he taught me; it helped me to be freer in my life and my art. It's important to visualize a positive future."

And part of that future will involve paying it forward by passing the torch to another generation. In accordance with Morrisseau's principles, Blair intends to give his gifts away when the time is right.

"Carry on what I'm doing when I'm dead, Morrisseau told me. When I die, continue to paint the bright colours; don't mutate them. Be bold and daring."

Although he still struggles at times, Blair works to eliminate negative emotions from his life. "I am learning to accept myself and love myself," he concluded. "I am learning that you have to give to grow."

He also works to deepen his understanding of Ojibway traditions and to refine his techniques.

"As I learn more, the art will change," he suggested. "And I will learn to touch the soul more deeply as we go on."

Today he takes comfort in his memories of Morrisseau as he creates colourful canvases that celebrate the songs, ceremonies and symbols of his heritage.

"We're born artists," Blair said. "The ideas come from our culture and from our own self-learning. We paint it as we feel it, but it is important to get it right for our people."

"Morrisseau believes that everybody can be an Indian.
Everybody has the potential to see the world through Indian eyes.
Just as everyone is born a Shaman but soon forgets."

-from an essay by Armand Garnet Ruffo accompanying the Norval Morrisseau, Shaman Artist exhibition, National Gallery of Canada, 2006.

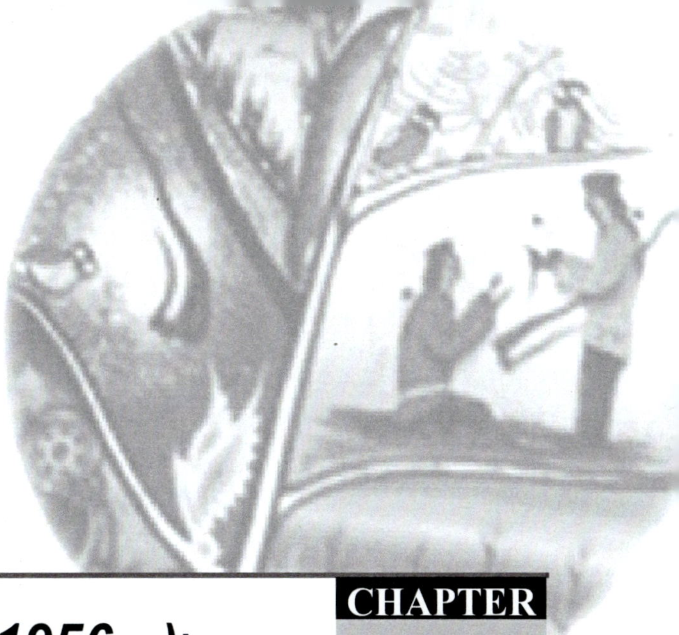

CHAPTER 6

BLAKE DEBASSIGE (1956 -):
Portrait of the Artist as Dragon Slayer

Many artists prefer to live quiet lives cloistered away in their studios, insulated from politics and social upheaval. And others choose to speak out against injustice and cultural appropriation. For Manitoulin artist, Blake Debassige, ignoring unsettling trends would be intolerable. Throughout his career he has remained a staunch protector of the environment as well as a vocal critic of the art establishment.

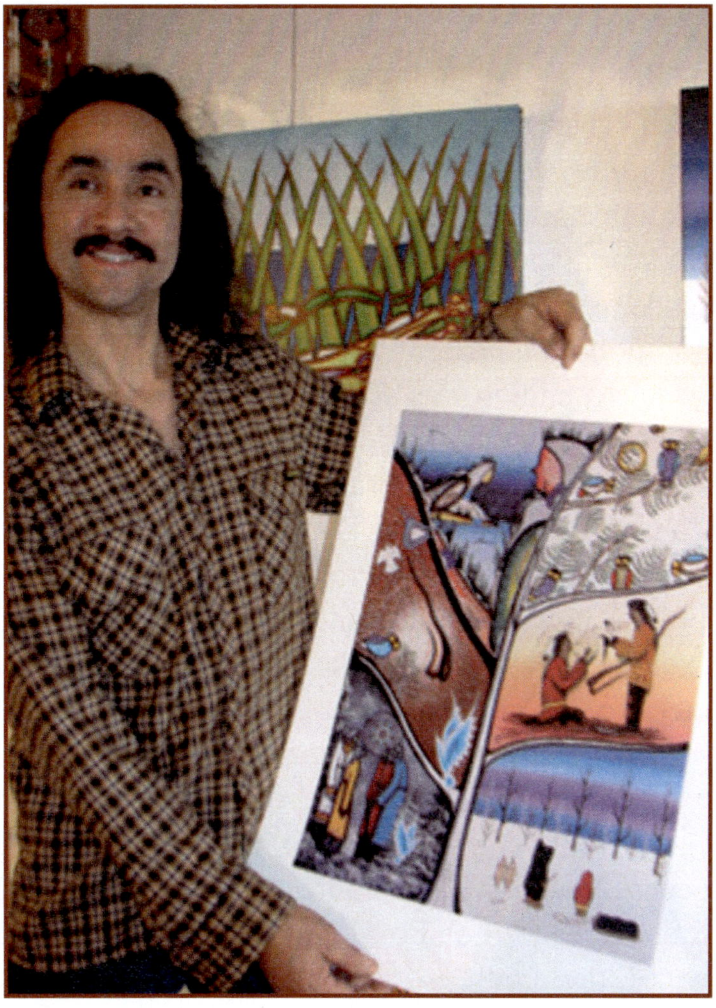

Blake was born in 1956, and grew up in the small central Manitoulin community of West Bay (now known as M'Chigeeng First Nation). Watching his father and his uncles paint inspired him to take up the brush and dabble in enamel paint as an eight year old. By the age of sixteen he had mounted his first public exhibition.

As a student at Manitoulin Secondary School (MSS) in the 70s, he describes himself as a fairly innocent youth when he was first introduced to European art history.

"In those days, I was naive; I just loved doing art. The politics would come later," he said.

In his formative years, he was content to explore and experiment with various techniques used by European masters, such as Pablo Picasso and Salvador Dali. He was particularly entranced by the significance of dreams in surrealist art forms. Looking back, he recognized that Picasso borrowed heavily from indigenous African art techniques.

During this time, he also had an influential encounter with Carl Ray, an Anishinaabe artist from Sandy Lake. Their meeting sparked a productive period of research and self-discovery. "When Carl came into our classroom, it was as if someone had turned on a light switch for me," Blake said. "I thought, wow, this is an amazing style; here was a style that wasn't of the European tradition. I could see that we had our own language, our own style. After meeting with Carl, I felt a need to learn more about the new style I had just witnessed."

Blake visited the school library and studied Dewdney's documentation of Midewin scrolls and petroglyphs. The research spurred him to journey even deeper into Anishinaabe art traditions.

The style he was gravitating towards as a youth had been dubbed the Woodland School of Art. In the years to come he would come full circle in his almost love/hate relationship with the term. There were times when he rejected being pigeon-holed into the Woodland School, because it had become a derogatory term to some art critics and academic instructors. At other times he declared himself proud to embrace the Woodland traditions and he fiercely defended the art form against all of its detractors.

Attending the Schreiber Island summer art camp established by Tom Peltier of Wikwemikong, also reinforced his resolve to deepen his knowledge and hone his skills. At the remote venue in the North Channel, he was tutored by pioneers in Native Canadian art, including Daphne Odjig, the Wikwemikong artist who blazed a trail for an entire generation of First Nations artists.

Knowledge acquisition went hand in hand with the growth of the art in those exciting times. For him the art and the stories were all intertwined, and the Elders he met in Wikwemikong whetted his hunger to delve deeper into the cultural teachings.

"I received a lot of stories and legends from people in Wikwemikong," he noted. "I used many of them in my paintings."

Summer projects at the fledgling Ojibwe Cultural Foundation (OCF) in M'Chigeeng, gave him even more opportunities to explore. Under the supervision of OCF founder, Mary Lou Fox-Radulovich, a dozen First Nations youth conducted interviews with Elders, gathered traditional recipes and natural remedies. Blake was called upon to do the illustrations for the recipe book of tasty *Anishinaabe Delights.*

The summer excursions provided many informal learning experiences for the young apprentices.

"We learned how to pick sweet-grass, how to make corn soup and sucker head soup," he recalled. "We visited Wikwemikong and Sagamok to interview medicine people."

These encounters were rare at that time because many of the medicine people were nervous about Health Canada's attempts to scrutinize and control their traditional practices, he added.

Although it was tempting to travel to other regions to study and paint, Blake chose to immerse himself in the indigenous knowledge present in his homeland.

"I was born and raised in the bush in Northern Ontario, not downtown Ottawa or Toronto or Vancouver. I became self-educated," he said. "As a result, my work is authentic, unadulterated, truly of the Manitoulin area. My images are not overshadowed by the motifs of New Mexico, Arizona, California or British Columbia."

This independent spirit has not always been appreciated, he acknowledged. In order to develop his own unique style, he has been forced to resist the efforts of authority figures to control his vision. He believes many art instructors try to steer budding artists into European conventions and rules. He recalled one particular class he enrolled in during a March Break from school. The session left him feeling stymied, judged and misdirected.

"I came away from that experience insulted and angry," he said. "The teacher tried to force me to be a puppet or a copy cat. She didn't know where I was coming from or what I was doing. She didn't recognize that I had my own distinct style."

In his view, a First Nations artist has a duty to combat that kind of coercion in mainstream art classes. "You don't have to paint like a white man to be legitimate," he stated. "The danger of art schools is that the professors tend to push their own agendas."

Over the past four decades the naive and curious youth has been transformed and the politicized and mature adult has emerged.

Being true to his roots did not bring Blake universal praise or exhibitions in the Toronto, Ottawa or Vancouver hot spots. Instead, he contends that Native artists continued to be burdened with damaging and restrictive stereotypes throughout the 1970s and well into the 1990s. Some critics dismissed Aboriginal art as suitable only for ethnographic institutions such as the Royal Ontario Museum.

"Many famous curators had contempt for the Woodland style," he suggested. "They said it wasn't art and labelled it as touristy and commercial. Some Ivory Tower elitists saw it as the last gasp of a dying race so they kept it out of the mainstream."

Looking back, he remembers the sting of the attacks and the ambivalence he felt about being labelled Woodland School.

"Many curators (and academics) said derogatory things about our art; many of them ridiculed and belittled it, especially in the early 90s," he recalled.

The mantle of the Woodland masters was both a blessing and a curse at times. It was a blessing to follow in the footsteps of the renowned Norval Morrisseau, the father of the Woodland style. And yet it was a curse to be blocked from prestigious national galleries. From Blake's vantage point, a system of "cultural apartheid" was still very strong in North America.

Surprisingly, some well-educated First Nations writers dismissed the Woodland work as well. According to Blake, "It used to be a running joke in artist groups about the 'woodpecker school of art.' It became a dirty word. Native artists were shunted aside and often deemed insignificant."

Such attitudes made it even more difficult for artists straddling two cultures to achieve recognition.

"In the past, people tended to lump all the Woodland School artists all together," he observed. "All Woodland artists were painted with a very wide, very white brush. I still feel as a Woodland painter that we have been left behind in the art ghetto."

Although the dismissive judgments were hurtful and discouraging, he spoke out against the perceived prejudice.

"I was totally against that bias," he emphasized. "I always stood up for our art as relevant as any other art form in the world. Our art is more spiritual than any other art form in the world except perhaps Africa and Australia."

He credits the McMichael Gallery for being the first public institution to promote Aboriginal painting as an art form and not an ethnographic curiosity. Over the years he has worked as artist-in-residence at the Kleinburg gallery and exhibited his work in England, Germany, Denmark and the United States. Collectors from all over the globe have visited his studio and gallery on Manitoulin.

If the 1970s were devoted to cultural immersion, the 1980s might be described as a time of evolving social consciousness. Blake continued to explore the nature of the cosmic order, the cycles of the seasons and the interdependence of animal, plant and human life. But he also moved beyond the nostalgia and romanticism that curators often associated with Aboriginal art. Bold, thought-provoking canvases addressed issues such as environmental destruction, cultural appropriation, youth alienation and suicide.

Ojibwe legends fired his creative imagination. For example, *Birch Woman (1982)* illustrates the legend of the Great Flood, an Anishinaabe creation story. In the same year he also produced *The Lonely Vigil* depicting a youth vision quest at Dreamer's Rock, another popular site for summer art camps.

Birds have always been a favoured subject. In 1993 he paid homage to the story of the robin, the bird that serves as the universal symbol for the return of spring. The sight of a magnificent owl perched on his red pick-up truck inspired him to capture its essence in a work entitled, *Snowy Owl*. Another commissioned piece celebrates the piliated woodpecker, a species once thought extinct. *Dorothy C*, is a loving tribute to the kindness of a former neighbour and caregiver in M'Chigeeng. The 1992 painting was inspired by a photo of a 13 year old girl visited by a chickadee on the window sill.

The decline of the bird population due to West Nile virus was certainly paramount in his mind when he produced the work entitled, *West Nile*, in 2005.

"I have been concerned about the number of dead birds that have been found and the fact that the virus was detected in M'Chigeeng," he explained. "But recently I noticed the birds are coming back so, hopefully, the West Nile has run its course."

Another virus that has definitely not run its course is HIV. Blake was deeply affected by the death of a close friend and colleague who had suffered from *AIDS*. He explored his unsettled feelings in a 2006 canvas, simply called, *AIDS*.

"When I visited him in hospital, the image was burned into my brain," he confided. "I was so shocked by his image. I was able to do some sketches then, but I had to leave it unfinished for a while. Later, I came back to it and I finished it."

Blake has been in the forefront of raising awareness of environmental degradation in recent years. For instance, his painting of the vanishing sturgeon reminds viewers that the dinosaur-like creatures once ruled the Great Lakes. But in the 1800s, many commercial fishermen killed as many of them as they could to use as firewood in the steamers that plied the lakes.

Reports of dead lakes in the Killarney area, prompted him to tackle water quality issues in a work aptly titled, *Acid Rain* (1985). By 2005, he had joined fifty other artists in an American art show exploring Native people's relationship to the Earth and the planet's energy crisis. He contributed a painting called, *Mother Earth's Presence*, to the Impacted Nations travelling show.

Natural Medicine, a painting of blueberries completed in 2005, underscores his advocacy of natural remedies and healing methods. Witnessing his grandmother's stressful ongoing struggle with renal dialysis, convinced him that people should look to nature for answers. It was difficult for him to stand by and watch his grandmother consume thirty pills a day to keep her going.

"We need to think more of preventative medicine and to stop eating processed foods," he stressed. "We need to be more conscious of healthy eating and preventing sickness and disease."

But Blake's work does not always spring from outrage or protest; sometimes he paints for the sheer joy of it. His pleasure in natural beauty shines through in works such as, *The Roses are Watching* or *Wild Grape Spirit* (1990).

Although he may appear to be somewhat harsh or cynical to those who don't know him well, Blake often reveals a sentimental and even romantic side. He can be a unrelenting critic, but he can also be a doting husband and father. This softer side is apparent in *Love Charms* (1983), which shows a profusion of wild roses in bloom while a young man plays the flute to win the attention of a young woman. This playful spirit is also seen in *Cree Indian Princess*, a work dedicated to his wife Shirley Cheechoo.

Naturally, he has collaborated on many music, film and drama projects with Shirley over the years. On one occasion he contributed *Lupi the Great White Wolf*, for a Debahjehmujig theatre promotion poster. And for Shirley's production of *Backroads*, he developed the imagery of *Bear Driving a Cadillac*. The film was later renamed *Bearwalker*.

Undoubtedly, the road to success has not been smooth, and recognition has been hard won, but in 1995 he was pleased to accept an honourary doctorate from Laurentian University in Sudbury.

Although there are still many closed doors, Blake has not forsaken his core beliefs. He is definitely not shy about taking on controversial issues. Being an activist and outspoken advocate for cultural integrity has always been part of his individualistic approach to art and life. He sees his job as an artist as very much in the legacy of the dragon slayer. Hypocrisy, fraud, deceit, forgery and disguise are all fair game for his arsenal of sarcasm, irony and parody.

An epidemic of a disease he calls "Grey Owl-itis," is spreading across the land, he has observed. It galls him to see "white Indians" wearing their "costumes" at pow wows, conferences and on television. He never misses an opportunity to poke fun at the Grey Owl wannabes in his midst. In a recent painting entitled *The Three Faces of Indians* he outlined three categories: full blood Indians, half-breeds and white Indians. In this scathing indictment of charlatans, he addressed the phenomenon of white people "masquerading as Indians to cash in on being Aboriginal."

He has often recounted the tale of one such encounter at his gallery in M'Chigeeng.

"Someone came to Kasheese to buy a gift for a shaman," he related. "Later I saw that the so-called shaman was really a white guy with braids."

Furthermore, Blake claimed that an-old-boy's-network and age-old misconceptions have blocked many First Nations artists from receiving grants and from gaining a foothold in sought after gallery spaces. He accused "fake Indians" in high level bureaucratic jobs, of shunning Native grant applicants and withholding funds from genuine Native artists. These gatekeepers monopolize all the plum jobs and hoard arts money for their cronies, he charged.

He has regularly condemned the policies of the Canada Council and the Ontario Arts Council, where applicants to funding programs are invited to "self-declare" their Aboriginal status. In his view, "This is a very scary trend. It is very favourable to be an Indian these days so many people are pretending to be Native."

Language preservation is another one of his top priorities. He worries about the watering down and the mis-teaching of the Ojibwe language in community schools. In their haste to make language instruction an integral part of the curriculum, administrators are relying on teachers who are not fully fluent.

"We need more teachers who have a full grasp of the nuances of the language," he stated. "Right now the teachers are not capable of properly instructing the children."

For him it is vital to "portray and represent the culture honestly and not do it for profit. Also it is important to teach our children and the rest of the world about our culture. We need to constantly dispel the image of the Hollywood Indian and wake people up to the appropriation of culture going on all around us."

Blake also regards the presence of fake medicine men as a danger. In his own community, he has witnessed the disturbing scene of a convicted paedophile directing a healing ceremony, shortly after release from prison. For Blake it is important to expose the "pseudo-spiritualists" marketing snake oil to the people of Manitoulin.

"A sex offender running a sweat lodge and offering spiritual guidance to youth. What's wrong with this picture?" he asked. His concerns about the "shady characters" have been underscored in a no-holds-barred painting he calls, *Shake 'n' Bake Shaman.*

As if phony healers weren't enough of an affront to moral sensibilities, theft of intellectual property is rampant as well. According to Blake, a flood of fake Woodland paintings appeared as soon as unscrupulous opportunists learned that renowned painter Norval Morrisseau was suffering from a debilitating illness.

"I want to speak out about this activity," he said. "Stealing is very prevalent. Once two Manitoba dealers offered me fake Morrisseaus at my gallery. I rejected them; I wouldn't touch them, but many fakes were sold here on the island. Public education is very important; people need to know about it (the theft). If a deal sounds too good to be true, it probably is."

Meanwhile, suits and countersuits are flying back and forth as some high profile galleries are forced to deal with the counterfeit masterpieces in their midst. Art experts have rushed to stem the tide of imitation Morrisseaus and an attempt is being made to catalogue all of the authentic products.

Other dishonesty strikes a little closer to home. Blake's own career has been affected by the "blatant fraud" and outright plagiarism committed by other would-be artists.

"I have created and developed my own system of symbols over thirty years," he told a gathering at the OCF in 2007. "And now people are blatantly ripping off my work and stealing my ideas."

Whether he's wearing the mantle of environmental crusader or whistle-blower at large, Blake takes his role as a dragon slayer seriously.

"It is important for artists to document the culture, to hold up a mirror on society and to speak out against injustice," he said.

As for his misgivings about the Woodland School, he no longer has any doubts about where he came from or where he belongs. In 2007, he affirmed anew his respect for the Woodland School legacy in a discussion of his work at the OCF. He paid tribute to mentors such as Carl Ray, Jackson Beardy, Saul Williams and Daphne Odjig. Like many young First Nations artists in the 1970s, he immersed himself in illustrating legends, but as his artistic vision matured, he developed his own unique style and mode of expression. When he encounters ignorance and prejudice, he remembers that even Canadian icons like the Group of Seven members were "dragged through the coals" and people joked about them. But now they are the quintessential Canadian art, he pointed out. He maintains faith in his process and his origins despite the frequent setbacks.

"A lot of my inspiration came from 500 year old birchbark scrolls and Agawa Canyon petroglyphs," he reiterated. "We experienced a Renaissance in the 70s and it belongs to us as a people. It's part of our culture and always has been. It keeps us going today."

And when he shared his outlook with listeners at a Laurentian University symposium in fall 2007, he again emphasized his roots in the Woodland tradition.

"I'm very proud of the Woodland School," he said. "I'm from the Woodland. The Woodland School has a long history, thousands of years, in fact. Yet, our culture is not frozen in time; it is not frozen in a nice little vignette. Change is constant."

He acknowledged that in the past he may have avoided the term because a whole group of artists were tarred with the same brush. So many in the art establishment failed to recognize First Nations artists as contemporary artists.

"Today I want to re-own the term," he said.

He went on to chastise the curators and critics who belittled Anishinaabe artists and treated them with a double standard over the past three decades.

"I am very proud to be an Anishinaabe," he stated. "Artists like myself are certainly not ashamed of their culture; they are certainly not ashamed of their language. That's who we are. We don't do American modernism. We don't need to emulate others; we have our own heroes."

He conceded that the residential school experiences combined with assimilation tactics have been devastating to some aspects of Anishinaabe culture. "However, the culture is still alive, the ceremonies are still alive; we are still fighting. Our warriors are still among us; they don't ride horses or throw lances, but they are still among us."

In closing, he urged the other artists at the Laurentian gathering to assert themselves and throw off decades of exclusion.

"A shot has been fired across the bow," he said. "It is up to the Aboriginal contemporary artists to take up the challenge."

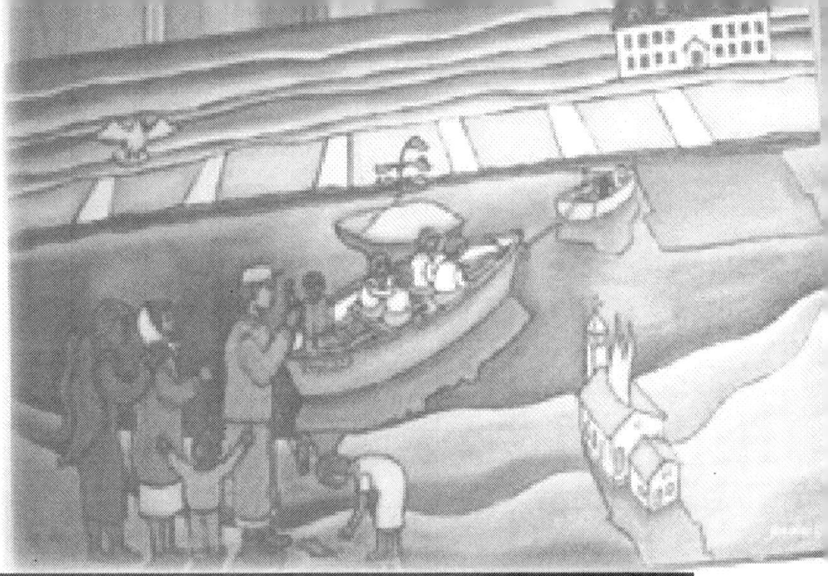

DON ENSE (1953 -): Drawing Upon Childhood Memories

CHAPTER 7

Like many of the young Anishinaabe artists who emerged in the 1970s, Don Ense explored both Woodland School conventions as well as European traditions before developing a style that was distinctively his own.He dabbled in fine art at Cambrian College (1974), and he travelled to artists' havens in Canada and the American Southwest. In the end, he discovered that the knowledge and the answers he sought were much closer to home.

His art draws upon memories of growing up in a large M'Chigeeng First Nation family that fished the lakes, made communal gardens, hunted wild game and worked in the bush. In many of his works, he has recreated activities involving his extended family, including six brothers and four sisters.

For Don, reading comic books as a child served as a spark to his imagination. At age eight, he was drawing cartoons with his uncle, Greg Ense and creating an animated comic book.

"I was taught the basics of art in elementary school," he said. "And all through my teens I continued to draw sporadically. I drew in a realistic style then and I have basically taught myself by studying art books."

Visits to museums and galleries expanded his horizons. On his own initiative, he studied library books on Pablo Picasso, Paul Cezanne, William Kurelek, Emily Carr and Allen Sapp. He absorbed the elements of Impressionism, Expressionism and Cubism that appealed to him, but for the most part, he learned from living artists he met on Manitoulin Island. As he searched for his own individual mode of expression, he would eventually try his hand at pottery, silkscreen, water colour and linocuts.

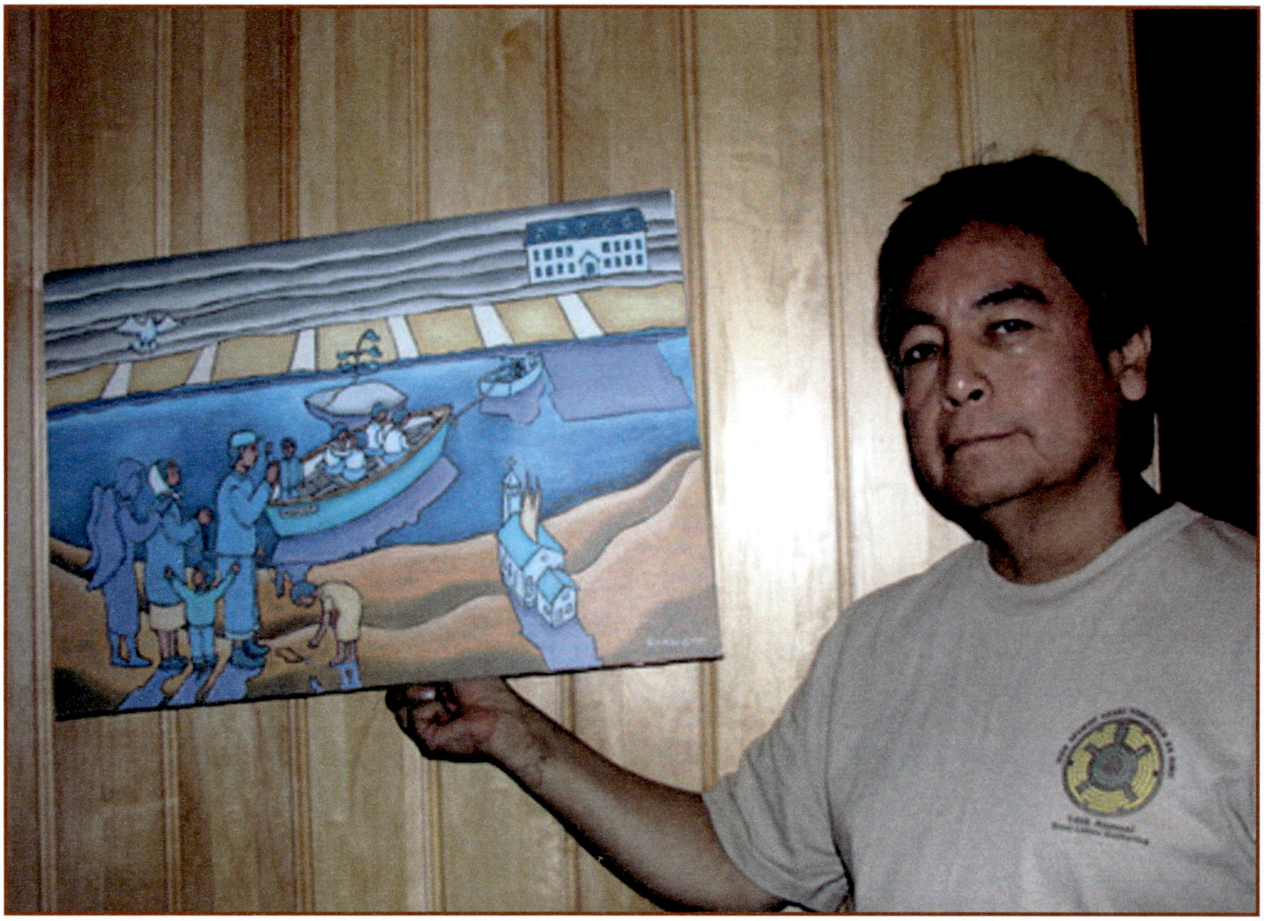

It seemed natural for a novice artist to gravitate towards the legend painting in that era. Don too, experimented with the Norval Morrisseau style which was very much in vogue with his contemporaries. In fact, he was fortunate to have an accomplished M'Chigeeng artist, Martin Panamick, take him under his wing in 1974 and help him make his first sale. Don speaks affectionately of his mentor who died tragically in a traffic accident at age twenty three.

"I grew up with Martin Panamick and I studied at his home studio for a year," he said. "That was a very productive time. He encouraged me and introduced me to the use of acrylics. Also, I was able to get re-acquainted with my culture."

Participation in the Ojibwe Cultural Foundation summer art camps in 1977-1978 also satisfied his thirst for more knowledge of the First Nations teachings and legends. The Birch Island gatherings provided an exciting environment for Don and fellow campers such as Randy Trudeau, Mel Madahbee, Blake Debassige and James Simon.

"At Dreamer's Rock, I met Stanley Redbird, a medicine man from South Dakota," Don recalled. "I had my first sweat lodge experience there and I was introduced to many other aspects of my culture. At that time I didn't know how it would play out in later years. Looking back in retrospect, I realize it had an impact on my later work."

Perhaps his most life-altering encounter came when he was twenty four. He sought the guidance of Carl Beam, an artist already making a name for himself as an unconventional artist. Don's inner instincts were affirmed when he witnessed Carl's steadfast refusal to be pigeon-holed.

"After talking with Carl, I made the decision to switch back to Realism, and it was the best decision I ever made," he said. "I departed from the Woodland style and I returned to my own realistic style. I made a complete break, yet I was still able to depict the Ojibwe philosophy and the values I was brought up to believe in. Carl showed me that it was okay to break the rules; I didn't have to follow the crowd."

As his confidence grew, Don was asked to illustrate publications such as *Dancing Feathers* and *A Time to be Brave* with Keitsch, Christel and Paul Stephens, (Annick Press 1985). He also provided the illustrations for *The Friends of God: Joseph Chiwatenhwa and Maria Aonetta*, by Bruce Henry. The Thunder Bay Art Gallery, Northern Affairs Canada and the Royal Ontario Museum added his work to their permanent collections. In addition, his approach was gaining favour with private collectors.

Additional success came when Don resolved to tap into his past where he discovered a well of inspiration for his unique art. He returned in memory to his favourite subjects: vignettes of family and village life on Manitoulin Island.

"I remember the day-to-day activities that I experienced as a child and these memories are just as important to the creative process as the visual subject," he noted. "When I paint my childhood memories, they serve as a metaphor for the various issues that affect my cultural identity as a North American Indian. It is reaffirming and rejuvenating to express my inner being."

He chose blue, yellow, red, brown and grey for his palette and painted the vital communal activities of his youth. In the process, he reinforced traditional values and preserved a vanishing way of life.

For example, paintings such as *Ice Fishing* (1978), highlight the importance of everyone pitching in to provide sustenance for the family. It shows Don and his brother, Stewart, on a frozen lake working to bring in the catch of the day.

"This scene depicts the closeness of family," he said. "Looking back it's the interconnectedness that I appreciate. There was a lot of interaction and every member had a function either as teacher or as student. We all helped to make the shelter at the fishing hole. The emphasis was on co-operation; we would all work together."

The special bond between generations is celebrated in *Setting the Net*, as well. The painting of Don and his grandfather in a home-made boat, pays tribute to the gifted craftsman and fisherman.

"He was my mentor in childhood," Don said. "He taught me how to fish, to hunt and to gather herbs. I was the oldest grandson so I would help him with a lot of tasks, particularly fishing. It was a main staple of our diet at that time. We would catch bass, whitefish, pike, trout and, occasionally, sturgeon."

The necessity of passing survival skills and traditions from one generation to the next has been a recurring theme in his art. This message is reiterated in *Hand Made Quilt*, a mixed media piece depicting his mother, teaching his sister, Molly, the finer points of blanket making. Through such simple tasks, the cultural traditions are kept alive.

Family members are also drawn with respect and dignity in a piece entitled *Wash Day*. This painting conjures up a domestic tableau reminiscent of the 1960s. In the intimate scene, the mother is washing her son in a tub in the kitchen while sister waits nearby for her turn to bathe. Nearby the bath water is heating up on a wood stove.

Reverence for nature's bounty is another value expressed throughout Don's body of work. In *Picking Blueberries*, the mother and daughter gather what the Earth offers for sustenance. Again the Elder passes along the knowledge and the tradition to the child. In *Syrup Making*, a similar kind of sharing process is evident.

In a companion piece, two youngsters are busy hauling water in two makeshift buckets fashioned from Tenderflake lard pails. Their father has given them a sometimes arduous household chore, but instead of complaining, the siblings seem to be having fun on a warm summer day. The *Two Children by the Lake* are Don and his sister, Molly.

When Don revisits some of his earlier canvases, he sometimes discerns new layers of meaning and comes to a deeper understanding of his formative experiences. Although he regards his upbringing with a measure of nostalgia, he is increasingly conscious of the hardships of subsistence living. With ten children being raised in a one room clap-board house, it was, by his own account, somewhat chaotic. Resources were scarce, but when he paints his memories, he dwells upon the warm familial connections and not the underlying sacrifices.

Children often exhibit a remarkable resilience and creativity in the face of deprivation. In *My Sister Molly*, Don celebrates the innocense of childhood and the ability of children to surmount and survive damaging circumstances by entering a dream or fantasy world. The painting also illustrates the Ojibwe tradition of using dreams as guidance for direction in life.

Dreams may have transported the Ense children to other possibilities many times over the years. When they were young, Don and his siblings, Shirley and Gary, invented their own amusements and games. One time they turned an old abandoned truck into a play area and a place for fantastic journeys. The painting entitled, *The Old Truck*, features a disabled vehicle up on blocks behind the house. As a youngster, Don got behind the wheel of that dark blue truck and travelled thousands of miles in his imagination. And he hasn't stopped yet.

"I was not aware of the poverty then," he confided. "I didn't realize the impact of poverty until later in life. I was just painting a realistic depiction of life. I was just painting how I saw it and how I felt it. I was not aware of the things we did without."

As his awareness of political and social issues has grown, he has produced a series of "protest paintings." A canvas entitled *Fear No Evil, Psalm 23,* is one of the powerful pieces in this category. It reminds viewers that the Canadian government used the Indian Act to forcibly remove Anishinabek children from their homes and place them in sterile residential schools. And it summons up memories of the precarious journey that students faced as flimsy boats carried them across Lake Huron to the church run school in Spanish. It captures the anguish of First Nations families coerced to relinquish their children to strangers who were determined to obliterate family and cultural ties. In one corner of the painting, flames can be seen shooting out of a burned out church.

Although the work protests the injustice of the archaic system, the overall message is uplifting. In Don's view, the fire represents renewal and an opportunity for healing. His own grandparents were sent to residential school and Don himself attended day school in M'Chigeeng, a harsh institution where the students were forbidden to speak their language. The symbolic torching of the church/school sets the stage for a new beginning.

"We need to go through a period of cleansing to purge us of the trauma of our history," he said.

The sense of hope is further underscored by the images of sunbeams, a dove and the comforting presence of an angel. Over the years he has witnessed many First Nations people meld tenets of Catholicism and Native spirituality to create a fusion of both belief systems.

"The church has always been a big influence in my life," he acknowledged. "Our family was Catholic, although my mother did eventually break from the Catholic church."

He refers to the blending of the two faiths in a painting entitled, *Ojibwe Nativity.* In echoes of the Biblical Christmas story, we observe an angel suspended over a babe in the manger while a mother beckons to her husband to come and witness the miracle. The animals in the stable stand in awe of the newborn. The overall atmosphere is warm, tender and accepting.

Environmental concerns are also addressed in Don's work. For instance, in *Mother Earth Crying* (1991), we see a tear falling from Mother Earth's eye and we feel the depth of her sorrow as she contemplates the loss of culture and the destruction of the planet. However, Don injects an element of hope into the scene. He envisions the eagle soaring high in the sky, always an enduring symbol of cultural resilience, perhaps an indication of his own personal resilience as well.

Like many artists, he has battled his own share of personal demons. He struggled with alcohol and drug issues at times, but entered recovery in the 1980s.

"I became aware of the need to deal with some of my issues," he said. "Part of that was to lean on the old ways to heal. When I did that, it became an intense period of change: I grew personally, spiritually and artistically."

As he gained insights into the roots of addiction, he was inspired to take courses in human services and sociology. Eventually, he went to work as a children's mental health worker for Native Child and Family Services in Toronto. As he helped people suffering from inter-generational trauma, he found that his art background was very valuable for reaching both adults and children.

"Art has been very therapeutic for me too; the process itself is healing," he acknowledged. "You go through all kinds of emotions when you paint; you experience a mixture of positive and negative feelings. And at the end of the process, it ends up being positive. It's like a pruning process where you let go of the old."

The Eagle and the Pipe, completed in 1991, transmits the hopeful message he has been sharing in his work and his relationships. It depicts the eagle carrying the prayers of the people to the Creator and it reiterates the principle that "everything is connected."

Clearly, the serene mood enveloping so many of Don Ense's paintings has been hard won. But with an artist's perspective, he has travelled back in memory to salvage the best of those bittersweet childhood days. He has been able to reach into the past and pare away the bitterness of poverty and oppression. Don has chosen to discard the negative times and treasure only the intangibles: love, compassion, tolerance and acceptance.

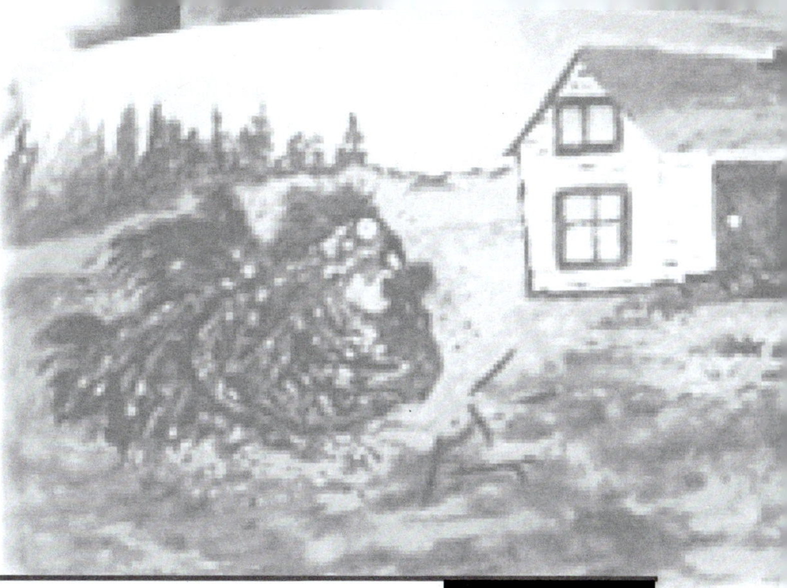

CHAPTER 8

FRANCIS PETER KAGIGE (1929 -): A Mystic and Visionary

Although the work of Francis Kagige is featured in many Canadian art collections, the pioneer Woodland artist lives a quiet and unassuming life on Manitoulin Island. A visit to his home and studio in Wikwemikong revealed that the octogenarian continues to create powerful imagery.

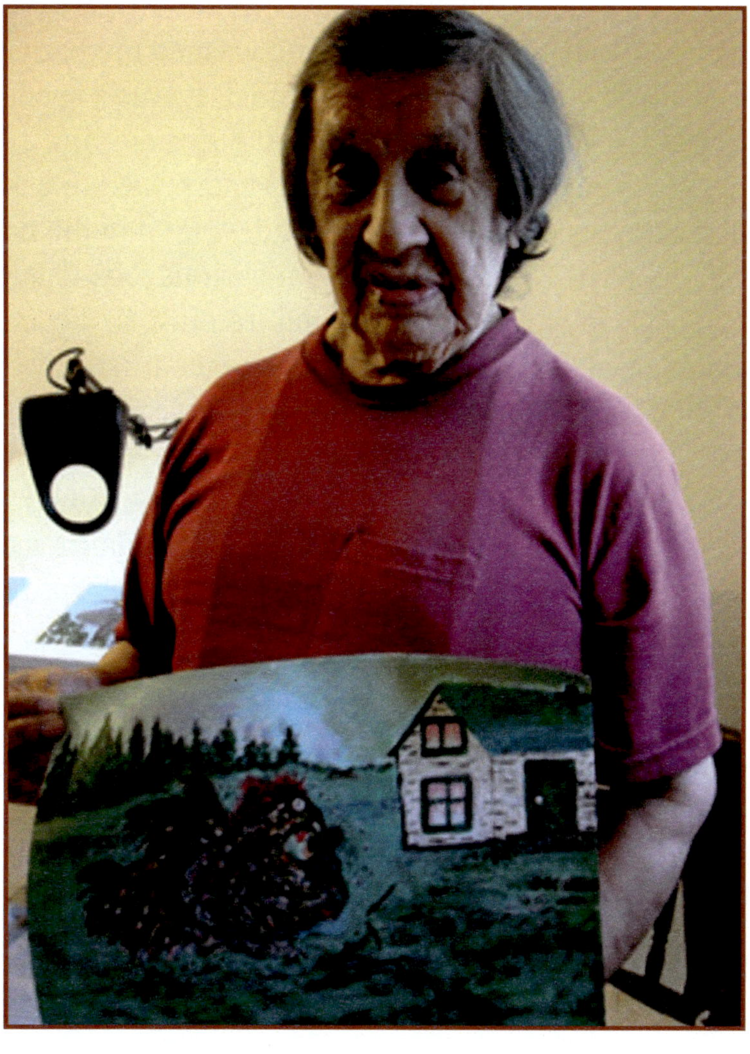

As he displayed several new paintings and related countless tales of his childhood and youth, it was clear that this Ojibwa Elder has a lifetime of inspirational experiences to share. No doubt his courage has been tested many times. Born in 1929, he experienced a debilitating affliction that kept him from walking until he was seven years old. During those difficult times he sought comfort in art and nature.

"The painting made me feel happy," he confided. "I did art from my dreams and my imagination. I listened to the sounds of nature all around me; I enjoyed hearing the jays and the orioles singing, the geese calling."

In school, Francis continued to find solace in art but it wasn't easy to practise his passion.

"It was really hard to get materials for art," he said. "So I used cardboard, birchbark and boxes."

One time, he cut his hand while crawling on the ground and he started sketching with his own blood. "I couldn't walk so I painted a rock with my blood, but the rock disappeared. Somebody took it. I was very disappointed," he added.

Despite the hardships, Francis has never downplayed the challenges he faced as a child. Instead, he has passed his life lessons on to others by depicting many of his formative experiences on canvas. For instance, in a recent work he drew a blue canopy suspended over black poles designed to protect a small youngster crouched in a washtub. An adult figure was shown in the midst of a healing ritual formulated to help the boy overcome partial paralysis.

"Nicholas Omnika, our neighbour, knew just what medicine to use," Francis recalled. "He boiled the roots and washed my body with the hot water in there. I started to walk two or three weeks after that. It was a special day and I have never forgotten it. It was one of the most important days of my life."

As he grew in strength, Francis was able to complete grade four. Eventually, however, he left the classroom and worked in the timber industry. Much of his adult life was spent in Toronto, working at various jobs to support himself and his art.

Despite the lack of formal training, he became a respected self-taught artist and visionary who influenced many younger artists, including today's masters, James Simon and Leland Bell. In the 1970s, critics were impressed by his distinctive formlines and x-ray interiors as well as the sinuous, organic contours of his traditional Anishnaabe symbols rendered in red, yellow, blue and brown. Writing in *The Sound of the Drum* (1984), author Beth Southcott praised his "flair for design in detail and his innate colour sense." She also observed that Francis Kagige has many imitators, but she dismissed the imitations as "second rate."

Forty years ago there was an explosion of interest in Aboriginal art and Francis was in the forefront of this surge of popularity. Despite his lack of formal education and training, he attracted support and attention from people who appreciated his mystical way of depicting First Nations legends.

"Solvis Westman of Toronto helped me a great deal," he said. "I had my first show in November, 1963 at the Toronto Art Forum."

Other Ontario shows followed that initial exposure. He exhibited at the First Unitarian Church in May, 1964, and at the International Institute, the Toronto Central

Library, the Japanese Cultural Centre, the Four Seasons Hotel and the Art Gallery of the University of Windsor, later that same year. In 1965 he participated in shows at Toronto City Hall and the Toronto YMCA. A display of his work was mounted at the Canada House Gallery, in Trafalgar Square, London, England in 1976.

When Canada's Expo 67 came along, it provided a great opportunity for Francis to showcase his work to an international audience. Wikwemikong cultural affairs consultant, Tom Peltier, invited Francis to help create a mural at the Indians of Canada Pavilion in Montreal.

As his reputation grew, he was invited to provide illustrations for *Tales of Nokomis*, by Patronella Johnston, published by Charles J. Musson Ltd. in 1975. And then in 1979, he contributed illustrations to *The Adventures of Nanabush: Ojibway Indian Stories*. He also illustrated Wilfred Pelletier's book, called, *Two Articles* and two of his paintings are shown in the book entitled, *I Am An Indian*.

Success continued during the 1980s. Francis participated in exhibitions at the Woodland Cultural Centre, in Brantford and the Thunder Bay Art Gallery. His work can be viewed in collections at the Canadian Museum of Civilization, Hull, Que., Indian and Northern Affairs Canada, Ottawa, ON, Institute of Alaska Native Arts, Fairbanks, Alaska, McMichael Canadian Art Collection, Kleinburg, ON, Royal Ontario Museum, Toronto, ON, Thunder Bay Art Gallery, Thunder Bay, ON and Lillian's Museum, M'Chigeeng, Manitoulin Island.

Since returning to his home community of Wikwemikong, Francis has been warmly welcomed by an entirely new generation of artists. Wasse-Abin High School named a student art award in his honour and invited him to act as a judge at the Manitoulin Mosaic Art Show in June 2008.

Francis continues to demonstrate affection for Wikwemikong, his birthplace. He is especially proud of a T-shirt design he created to celebrate his home community. Since Wikwemikong means "bay of beavers," Francis drew the shape of a large beaver with the letters of Wikwemikong running from the head to the tail. Above the beaver image, three stylized geese are flying, illuminated by his trademark sun logo. And below the animal outline, the words "Creator Island, Ont. are printed.

Settled comfortably into the seniors' residence behind the Wikwemikong Wellness Centre, Francis has taken a keen interest in local, national and global affairs. In a recent flurry of creativity he has produced paintings that explore social ills and recurring problems facing humanity.

For example, one of his works focussed on the scourge of addiction in many communities and underscored his concern for the well-being of modern youth. The message is all the more meaningful because he has battled his own demons in the past.

The unnerving canvas features a massive balloon-like head with penetrating eyes that seem to follow the viewer with an ominous stare. The disembodied brain is shrouded in a dense brown fog that leaves only a narrow mask around the eyes of the addict. The blank eyes that peer out from the mask are ultra white ovoids with tiny blue, dilated pupils. The huge head floats on a background of soft blue, overlaid with images from nature, including waterfowl, flowers, fish and owls. Human figures are shown mired in the chaos caused by alcohol and drug abuse. By capturing the glassy-eyed vacuum of the addict, Francis has made an attempt to reach the present generation.

"People are drinking too much," he stated. "This painting is a message to young people to stop taking drugs. I hope the young people can get help."

As Francis entered his 80s, the mysticism of his youth appeared undiminished and his powerful vision remained intact. He still freely described the travels he undertook in his dreams to distant times and past lives. In his painting of *The Buffalo and a Hunter*, for instance, he re-created a disturbing scene that took place on the North American plains in the aftermath of European contact. In the past, the buffalo herds were slaughtered and on the verge of extinction. However, Francis envisioned himself defending the noble animals. His work depicts the harried herd thundering across the land, accompanied by a brave young hunter astride a painted pony.

"In the past, I lived on the prairies," he said. "I was born again; I recognize places where I used to live. The white guys came and they shot the buffalo. They just killed them and the horses. They killed my horse too."

After all the tragedy he has witnessed in this life, Francis does not hesitate to express his opinions about current events. For example, he has always felt strongly about the presence of Canadian troops in Afghanistan. If he had a chance to speak with the leaders, he would share his misgivings.

"I would tell the Prime Minister to stop making war over there," he says. "I would tell them to stop making bombs and guns. All I want is peace and happiness."

And that is perhaps the greatest legacy of this soft-spoken artist. The youth of Wikwemikong and beyond can benefit from the positive teachings of this Manitoulin trail-blazer.

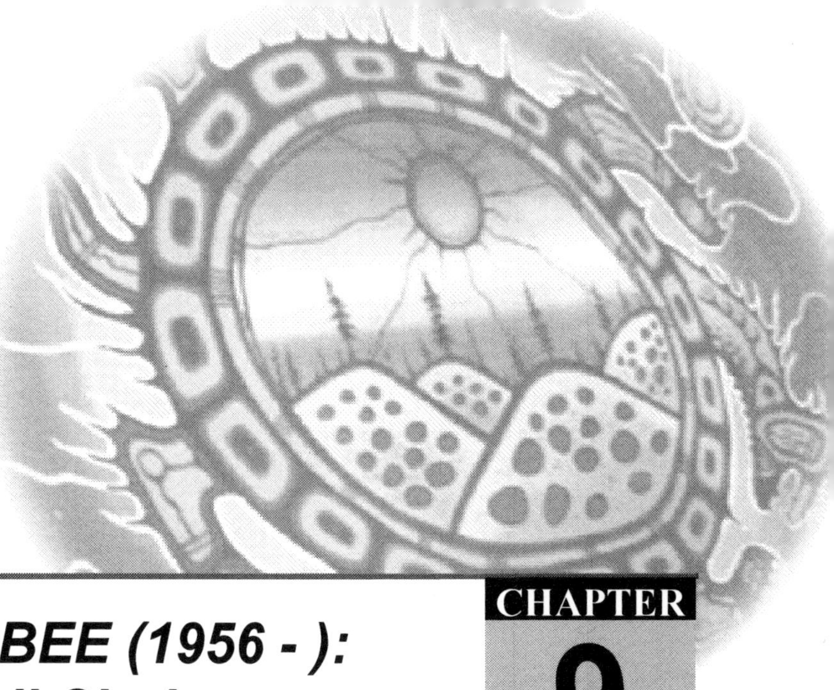

CHAPTER 9

MELVIN MADAHBEE (1956 -): Coming Full Circle

Many acclaimed artists have endured traumatic events or encountered overwhelming obstacles in their careers. Oftentimes the artist will emerge from a personal or health setback with a new vision or sense of purpose. For Melvin Madahbee, a member of the Ojibways of Sucker Creek, a series of medical crises have brought him full circle in his work.

When this writer visited him at his residence at Aundeck Omni Kaning First Nation in summer 2008, he and his wife Melvina greeted me with a smile and an eagerness to share his latest paintings. Melvin and Melvina have deep roots in the community and have travelled many miles together on the Red Road over the past three decades. They are proud that their own children have settled nearby and take great pleasure in their grandchildren.

Although Melvin had suffered a debilitating stroke three years before, he had made remarkable progress in rehabilitation. In his work space at his home, he had recently completed two paintings depicting an albino deer and he was in the process of planning a third canvas in the series.

This was an encouraging development for all concerned. In fall 2007 he had been invited to participate in the "Manitoulin Cross-Pollination Project", a writer/artist collaboration initiated by the Manitoulin Writers' Circle. During the project, a writer would share a poem or story with an artist and the artist would use the writing as a launching pad for a new piece of art. In turn, the writer would respond to the artist's existing works and produce a new fiction or non-fiction piece. The outcome of the co-operative venture was slated for exhibition at the Gore Bay Museum and Heritage Centre October 17, 18, and 19, 2008.

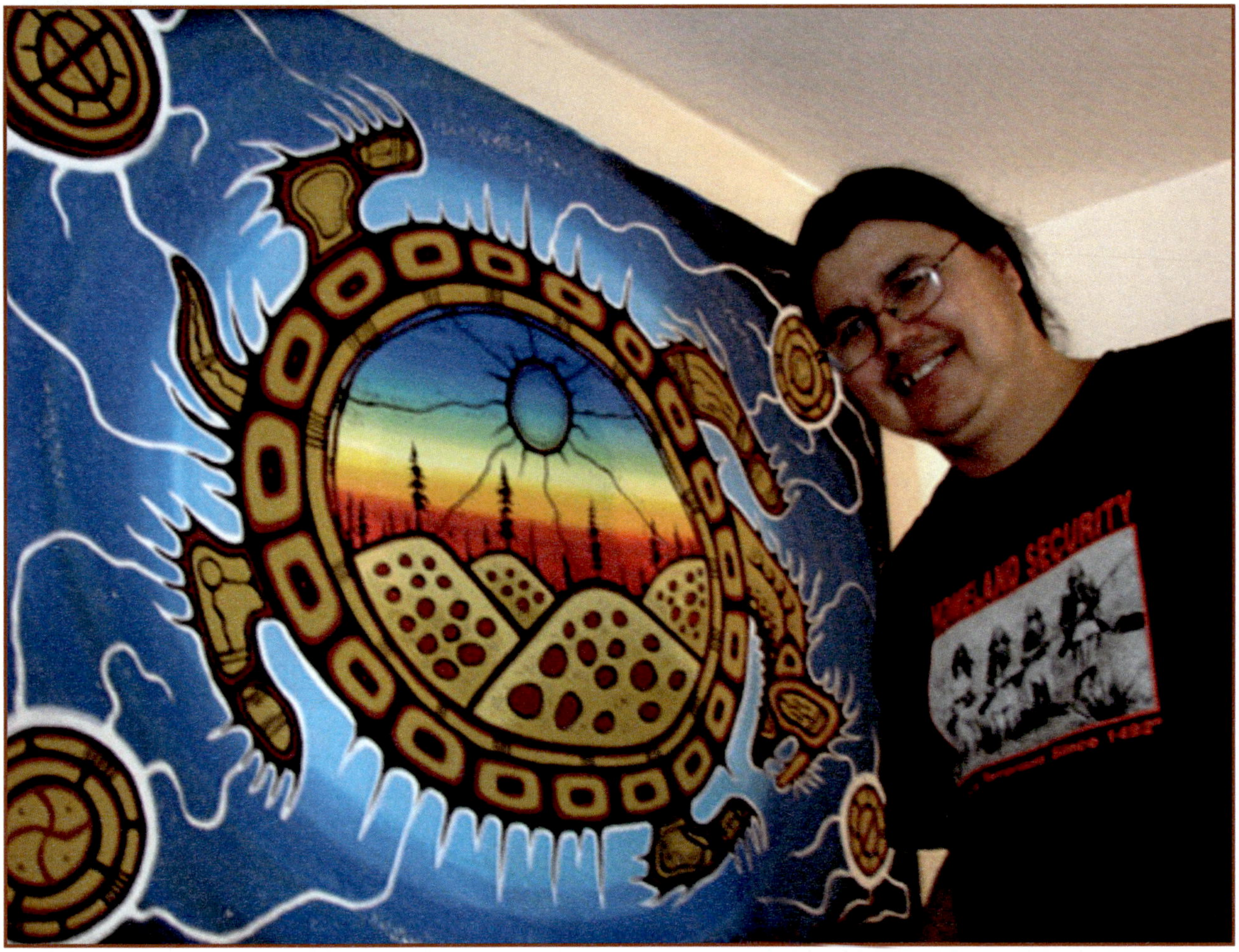

At first Melvin was reluctant to commit to the partnership because of on-going health issues. However, in May 2008, he had a change of heart. He had read a short story entitled, *The Manitoulin Ghost Deer* and was inspired to illustrate the tale. In the past, he had shown a great fondness for moose and deer portraits, producing works such as, *Mother Doe and Her Newborn*, *Little Deer Venturing* and *Autumn Deer*. So after he read the fictional account of a magical white deer, he felt motivated to start making a series of sketches.

In July 2008, as I paid a visit to his home studio, it was clear that he was experiencing a period of rejuvenation. He shared the story of his father's experience with a similar "ghost of the woods."

"My Dad had once shot a white deer," he said. "It got away so no one believed him. In the past there used to be white deer and white moose; the people believed that there was something sacred about the white buffalo and the white moose."

During a far ranging conversation, Melvin talked about the extensive body of work he had completed over the past thirty years. And he unabashedly described the mysterious collapse he survived on May, 26, 2005.

"I had been working on a painting called *Old Man on a Horse*, but I never got to finish it," he confided.

The day it happened, he had set out as usual, for his job feeding the rainbow trout at the Wabuno Fish Farms in Aundeck Omni Kaning. He had ridden his bike to the dock and boarded the boat that carries the employees to the site at East Rouse Island. Suddenly, he was gripped by a seizure and a partial paralysis that would leave his memory and perceptions permanently altered.

"Half of my body went on me," he recalled. "I couldn't use one side. And I couldn't tell anyone what was happening; it affected my speech and my memory. I had bitten a hole into my tongue and I couldn't talk. I almost forgot who I was, but they tell me I laughed through it all."

For the family that depended upon him for support, there was no humour to be found in the sudden collapse of their breadwinner and the near-drowning that followed. The catastrophe brought months of hardship and anxiety. Melvina acknowledged that the job had always been stressful because Mel was separated from his family for long hours and had to travel in "endless days of hazardous weather." Although they were happy he had a permanent job, she bemoaned the fact that "he missed about ten years of kids' parties and graduations."

As Melvin began a slow recovery, his wife coped with his "memory problems" by patiently cueing him and reminding him of events. "He often showed an over-exaggeration of humour," she noted.

And he is still laughing to this day, although this accident was not his first brush with mortality by any means. Since 1977, there have been at least four near-death experiences. One of the most critical incidents occurred in Kenora in 1986. At that time he had been commissioned to create a mural project at the school on the Whitedog First Nation.

For Melvin some of the details of that crash are as vivid as if it happened yesterday.

"I fell off of a sixteen foot ladder; I was holding a gallon of paint in my hand," he said. "I had broken my arm and the compound fracture couldn't be fixed in Kenora so they had to fly me to Winnipeg."

During his recovery, he started to attend pow wows and participated in men's traditional dance, acquiring his eagle bustle in 1986. He received funding from the Ontario Arts Council to serve as Artist in Residence at the White Dog Reserve in 1987 and the art continued to evolve and move in different directions.

Versatility and resilience have always been his strengths. Born July 27, 1956, in Blind River, Ontario, Melvin has been painting since the age of ten. He graduated from Manitoulin Secondary School in 1976 and took part in the summer art camps offered by the Ojibwe Cultural Foundation in the late 1970s and early 80s. He also participated in courses held at the Elliot Lake Art Centre and acquired a Fine Arts Certificate from Humber College, in Toronto. In addition, he became a talented cabinet maker through training at Cambrian College. In the early phase of his career, he was drawn to the work of wildlife artist, Glen Loates. During the 1960s and 70s, Melvin devoted himself to portraits of animals and natural beauty. He worked in a variety of media, including watercolour, enamel, oils, pencil, ink and acrylic.

"In the 70s, I was a landscape artist," he noted. "I was painting sceneries such as sunsets at Birch Island and Sunshine Alley. But around 1975, I quit doing sceneries and I switched to native (style) art."

The public was receptive to his diverse techniques and exhibitions at Tundra Gallery in Sault Ste. Marie, the Art Effects Gallery in Sudbury, the Royal Ontario Museum in Toronto and Turtle Gallery in Niagara Falls followed. He was also asked to participate in the Northern Lights Festival Boreal, the Manitoulin Trade Fair and Ojibwe Cultural Foundation shows. In addition, he joined fellow artist Leland Bell in teaching art in the classroom at Manitoulin Secondary School.

Indian and Northern Affairs Canada, the McMichael Canadian Collection, the Ojibwe Cultural Foundation and the Clarke Irwin Company currently treasure his works in their permanent collections.

Melvin was also part of the "Manitou Collection: Celebrating the Spirit of the People", a touring exhibition organized by the WKP Kennedy Public Art Gallery and the Manitou Conference of the United Church of Canada. The show toured Northern Ontario in 2006 to mark the 20th anniversary of the United Church of Canada's first official apology to First Nations peoples.

The Naandwegamik Health Centre commissioned him to paint their logo which was prominently displayed in the hub of Aundeck Omni Kaning.

For Melvin the renewed flurry of creativity in the summer of 2008 was a sign of hope. It was an indication that he had come full circle as an artist. Although the illness had changed his memory and perceptions, possibly forever, he had adapted and accepted the gifts inherent in this new phase of his life journey. It is a joy to hear him laugh frequently and to see him painting for the sheer joy of it.

"It's opening up a different chapter in my life," he said. "I am starting to do the sceneries again; it's what I started out doing when I was young. I am enjoying the work I'm doing now; it's opening up new doors, at least that's what it feels like."

Melvina also viewed the the Manitoulin Cross-pollination Project, as a fortuitous opportunity for the family. "The project gave Mel a reason to thrust forward with his art," she observed. "And it resulted in a spectacular outcome of rejuvenation."

The presence of Melvin at traditional pow wows throughout Manitoulin is further evidence of his "joie de vivre." Since he had a new artificial valve installed in his heart, he has resumed traditional dancing. For him, dancing is a way to celebrate sobriety and to thank the Creator for the gift of each day.

"I have been drug and alcohol free for twenty five years now," he said. "It's important to keep dancing. It feels good to move around and to be free of all that. It feels good in the heart."

He has gone on to share those good feelings with the community during Youth and Elders gatherings at the OCF. In workshops showcasing Anishinaabe art he passes on his positive outlook and his innovative techniques.

His home community recognized his contributions at the Aundeck Omni Kaning "People's Choice Awards," held on January 14, 2009. The event, sponsored by the band's health and social services agencies, was instituted to enhance community spirit.

Although Melvin is aware that catastrophe can happen out of the blue and that many things in life are beyond control, he greets each day with gratitude. In his art and in his dancing, he shows the world his indomitable, invincible spirit.

Melvina agrees the recovery has been nothing short of miraculous. "It has been three and a half years since the stroke and again Mel seems to be bucking the odds of having any disability from the traumatic attack to his brain," she said. "Of course, we still have to monitor the (mechanical) heart valve that was installed during an operation for an enlarged heart. And the irreparable damage to the brain has taken a lot of memory, but I think Melvin's setbacks only made him stronger to do even better. As you watch and figure out what he's doing, you realize his paintings express all the totality of creation and life."

Witnessing her husband's struggle to regain his language skills and practise his art has given Melvina hope and a sense of purpose.

"Just watching his daily activities, shows one a caring and nurturing soul that makes one feel positive and energized. But I do wish for people to be aware of what a stroke can do to a person and their loved ones," she said. "So now I must become a voice for the voiceless or brain-injured persons for as long as I can."

DIAMOND-HEART DANCER

A Tribute to Melvin Madahbee by Margo Little

You have journeyed to death's door
You have fallen from great heights
You have plunged into frigid depths
Once you even lost the gift of speech
And grasped to catch fleeting memories
Yet you've never forgotten how to dance

Each time you battled back from the edge
You paused on the brink of the spirit world
Observing the world you were about to leave
And gazing upon the one beckoning to you

A team of surgeons fashioned a mechanical valve
Fortified your failing heart with man-made materials
That you might stay with us to paint and dance again

In full regalia, you dance to the drumbeat
Every movement a prayer of thanksgiving
The future remains for now uncertain
But in this present precious moment
You are diamond, you are invincible
A spirit unconquered by adversity
It feels good in the heart to dance

You who have glimpsed the world beyond
Have seen the universe in a different light
That clarity of vision now guides your steps
To spectacular scenes of winter's storms
To autumn deer resting by peaceful waters
And to summer's eagles soaring skyward

Dance, Diamond-Heart Man
Your spirit shines, its lustre undiminished
Dance, Diamond-Heart Man
In the glow of a Manitoulin sunset

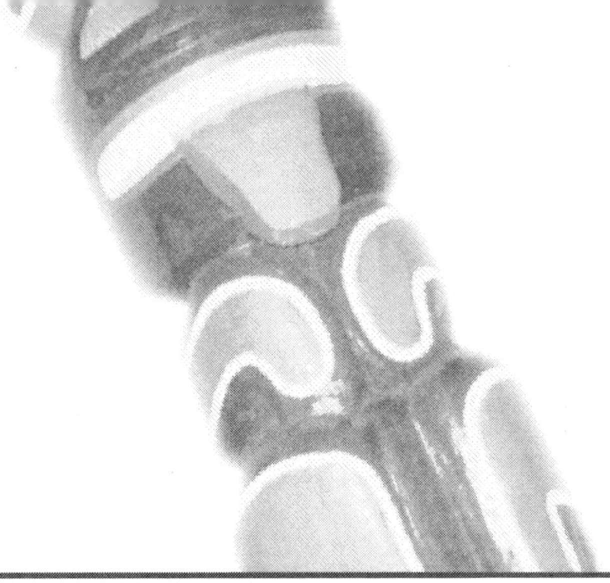

CHAPTER 10

DAVID MIGWANS (1960 -): Revelations in Clay and Canvas

Like many artists, David Migwans has experienced a long period of soul-searching and dislocation. Of Ojibwe-Odawa descent, he was born July 28, 1960 in West Bay. During the past four decades, he has struggled to overcome the residual effects of childhood trauma and to find his place in the world. The yearning to find stability and a satisfying mode of expression was always there even in the darkest times.

"I have been searching for what I have to give," he said simply.

In his early 20s, he started working with Carl Beam, one of his relations through the Migwans clan. Carl had spent some time in the southern United States learning pottery techniques. When he returned to Manitoulin, he took David under his wing and shared his own process of discovery.

"When I first started working with the clay in 1973, it was like I was made for it," David recalled. Of course, it was trial and error with the pots in the beginning. It was all experimental. I had to learn how much sand to add to the clay, how to heat it properly. If I made it too hot, if the heating process was too rapid, I would have to cry and pick up all the pieces. But Carl was there to advise me. He had a special way of explaining things."

In his troubled youth, David found comfort and validation in his relationship with Carl. His cousin talked openly about their upbringing steeped in violence and "nightmarish" childhood memories. There were "common threads" of alcoholism and assaults in their personal stories. Eventually, David began to understand that he needed to manage his rage and try to salvage some good memories from the past. It would take many years to put the painful ones into perspective.

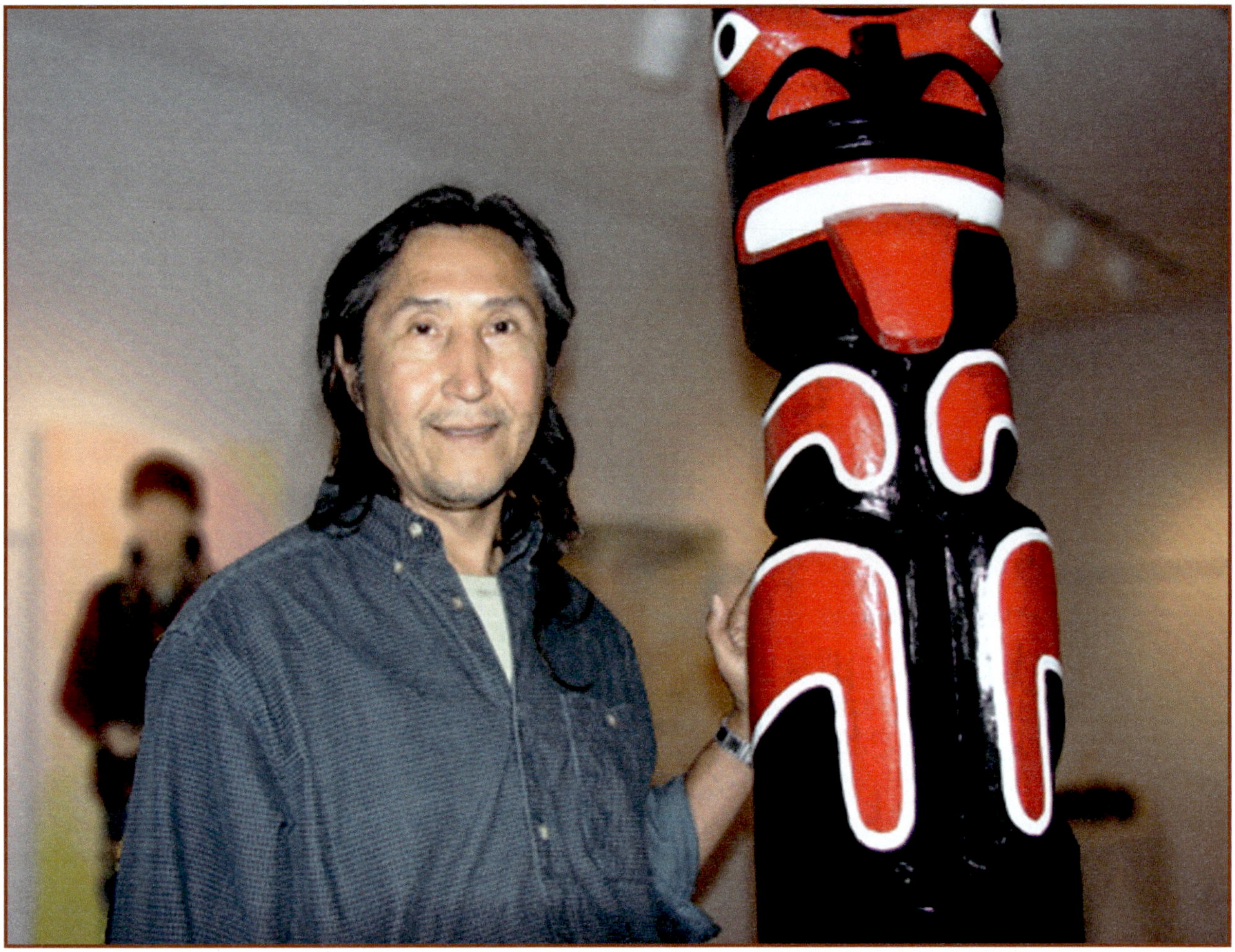

“I have real definite memories of my brother being angry with my father, of my brother stabbing my father in the arm, of my father beating my mother,” he confided. “I wasn’t as angry as my brother was, but there is still a residual anger in me. It’s necessary to exorcize the anger, to cut it out and put it on the table or it consumes you.”

As horrific as some of his remembrances are, David does not want to blot them out entirely. He believes it is important to remember everything that happened and not choose denial.

He left Manitoulin and journeyed to Montreal in 1982 hoping to discover just the right medium for self-expression, just the right way to live with his inner demons. For the next eleven years he would travel back and forth from Quebec to M’Chigeeng. Eventually he stopped straddling the two solitudes and moved home to open a studio and gallery in 1994.

He had always been close to his mother, Maime Migwans, a well-respected artist, and had inherited her gifts of persistence and self-discipline. He grew up watching her do the painstaking work required to create her beautiful porcupine quill boxes. He also participated in gathering of materials for her black ash basketry.

"When I was eight or nine, I had to hold the log still for my Dad while he pounded the bark, maybe five or six blows," he said. "Later I saw my mother making thin strips and separating the layers of bark to do her baskets."

Many years later, during a visit to the fabled Agawa Canyon rock paintings, he was reminded of his mother's stories. As he viewed the legendary Lake Superior water-spirit, he gained a new appreciation for the symbol that often appeared in his mother's artwork.

"At first you don't notice the image," he said. "It's not clearly visible, so it doesn't jump out at you. But it did have a big impact on me. It is very important to be respectful to the spirit and to be cautious about putting a meaning on it. I will leave the interpretation to the Elders. It's still a very deep mystery to me."

With the spirit image in mind, he set out to build a clay representation of the creature. He used earthenware clay from the Echo Bay area. After carefully screening the material to remove the pebbles, he created the hollow-bodied sculpture with the image of two canoeists, also reminiscent of Northern Ontario pictographs.

"When I fired it, I got it on the first try," he smiled with satisfaction.

In the past, producing pottery meant working with a wood fired kiln and very basic equipment. Cutting the wood made it a very labour intensive ritual. And there was always the danger you "could sear the hair off your arms." Later, he opted to use a safer, more efficient electric fired kiln.

The basic steps needed to mould the exquisite pottery haven't changed much since the 1970s. He still patiently screens the pebbles, roots and other impurities out of the earth before starting the coil-building method. The work is a gradual process as each individual coil is attached to a flat slab of clay which is held in a strong bottom support, such as a Chinese wok, lined with cheesecloth to prevent the clay pot from sticking to the metal. All the seams are smoothed over and the wall thicknesses are gauged "by feel alone." All of this requires much practise. Later, sanding removes the rougher exterior surfaces to allow painting.

When he makes pottery, David enjoys using traditional motifs such as flower or diamond patterns. But he always puts his own personal stamp on the objects he creates.

"It is important to put your own twist on it and to bring something of yourself to it," he stressed.

This approach is apparent in works exhibited in 2007. A series entitled, *The Seven Bowls of God's Anger*, reveals his on-going struggle to make sense of the turmoil plaguing Mother Earth. The ceramic vessels he created, correspond to the Biblical text revealed in the Book of Revelations.

"I have been exploring and building a personal belief system," he said. "I wanted to create a belief system I could call my own."

Since his parents were influenced by experiences in residential schools, David was raised with both Catholic and Ojibwe teachings. As an adult, he has studied both traditions in an attempt to define and articulate his own personal philosophy of life.

For David, the events described in the Book of Revelations, seemed to be an eerily accurate insight in modern day ills. In response to the readings, he designed the bowls to explain his interpretation. In essence, the bowls serve as a visual expression of the Biblical parables. And he didn't have to look too far to see evidence that many of the predictions have come to pass. Environmental degradation has even affected his once pristine and protected island.

"They (the prophecies) show the water turning bad," he said. "Because of the pollution, we have to filter our water now. As a kid I could scoop water right from the creeks to drink."

The revelations also outlined unpleasant realities that people of the 21st century have come to accept. Everywhere are signs of a warming planet as the intense heat of the sun burns the people and scorches the Earth. Widespread war, chaos and confusion disrupt the lives of ordinary people. Globally, ethnic and political groups use their power to conquer others and to force their ideology on their captives. In the process, the great cities of the world are crumbling.

In David's view, there are many modern parallels for the events engraved on the seven bowls.

"We see Muslims and Christians not being able to come together. They all want their religion to be the one and only one," he observed. "People get so fanatical about their beliefs. People are losing their way."

From his perspective, it is important for people to read widely and to think for themselves. As part of his self-education he has embraced aspects of both Catholicism and Ojibwe-Odawa spirituality. Viewers should not be surprised to see an image of Mother Theresa on one of his bowls on display. And they are certain to find unity symbols recurring throughout his body of work. A large work acquired by the McCord Museum in Montreal in the mid-80s, features figures all holding hands in a gesture of universal solidarity.

After viewing a David Migwans pottery exhibit, one is compelled to agree with the observations of poet/sculptor Ann Elizabeth Carson when she says, "the clay does not lie." And as critic Alex Jacobs wrote in *Akwekon* magazine (April 1986), "Clay is poetry in the discovery, the form, the design, the use, the prayers, the fire, the earth, the eye, the hand, the final place where the piece discovers itself and when we go, the clay will remain."

Fortunately, for the art world, David decided not to confine himself to strictly clay work. He turned his hand to painting and by 2003 he was an honours graduate of the Cambrian College fine arts program.

In a range of work exhibited in 2007, viewers can clearly see that David is well-acquainted with rage, with tears, with grief. But they can leave exhibition spaces knowing he is also in touch with hope, faith and forgiveness. In his intensely personal shows, he leads the viewer on a journey from the depths of despair to a vision of redemption.

The anguish of a young child caught up in family violence and alcoholism is illustrated with gut-wrenching realism in a painting entitled, *Woodland Nightmare*. This is not a sentimental or nostalgic coming-of-age story. Far from it. Instead, a child of perhaps four or five, is shown trying to survive the chaos around him, trying to guess at what is "normal." A small vulnerable figure clad in a red sweater and black pants makes eye contact with the spectators who pass by. One of the child's eyes is covered by a hand wiping away tears or perhaps trying to block out the horror he sees before him.

"This image stems from a very dark place," David revealed. "It shows the first house we lived in. We had a very old place; it was a pukey green house with holes in the walls."

In this canvas, David appears to harken back to the direction he received from his mentor, Carl Beam. His cousin had encouraged him to go beyond the sometimes confining limits of "Woodland art" and to resist labels in order to be a post-modern, contemporary artist.

David's *Woodland Nightmare*, is infused with disturbing images as seen through the eyes of a child forced to witness unspeakable events in his home. Streaks of dark red blood run down the green walls. The black holes in the walls seem to harbour all the pain of his existence.

"I saw a lady at the kitchen table; she was one of my sister's friends," he recalled. "She seemed sad, depressed. I saw her slit her wrists right there in front of me."

David remembers many days spent hiding under the bed to escape the sounds of punches and slaps and general "craziness." The searing images have haunted him in all his travels, in all his questing for peace and serenity.

"It brings back memories of the fights my Dad had with his friends at his house," he added. "It brings back memories of the dirty, pukey green house with the broken glass on the floor, the broken windows, the blood, the cops coming to the door."

It would seem inevitable that he would get lost, that he would be overwhelmed with resentment. Publications documenting the abuses at state-sanctioned and church-run residential schools further fanned his fury.

"I read that book about the residential schools and it made me very angry. I began to understand more about our parents' behaviour," he said. "My sisters and I suffered because of the residential school impacts. I still feel those impacts. The more I read, the angrier I got."

Historical research helped him develop empathy for his father and to gain insight into the roots of his addiction. He continues to educate himself about the system that left a scar on all of his siblings and cousins. From the stories passed down from the survivors, David concludes that the nuns and priests attempted to snuff out all the aspirations of the children in their charge.

"My father told me that he had a dream to be a doctor, but the nuns were full of ridicule. 'You'll never be nothing but a witch doctor,' they told him. I have every reason to be angry," David said.

Painting a large canvas entitled *Residential Schools and Inter-generational Impacts* (2003), was somewhat cathartic for him. He envisioned youngsters torching the schools to end the abuse, to stop the pain.

"I had heard stories about fires being set at the schools," he explained. "In my fantasy, I imagined how that would look."

In the multi-layered painting he shows a raging fire wiping out the school while the affected families rise above the rubble to be reborn and to reclaim their heritage. The flames purify the institution and cleanse away the injustice.

To the left of the canvas, he has placed his niece and her children as symbols of First Nations' families emerging from the ashes of the destructive system. They are lifted up, phoenix-like, no longer buried by the mainstream culture imposed by the clergy and the government.

Skulls, white crosses and white ghost figures hover in the background of the painting to represent the spirits of all the children who died while under the care of church officials. He also includes a figure meditating at Dreamer's Rock to signify that the Anishinabek are re-discovering their culture.

All along the bottom of the scene are beer bottles scattered about as evidence of the enduring scourge of addiction.

"Alcoholism was very prevalent; it was very harmful to families," he reiterated.

To underscore the message, the Canadian flag in the lower right corner is turned upside down as a universal symbol of distress.

Although the work was ignited by anger, the overall theme is essentially hopeful. The painting celebrates the tenacity, resilience and endurance of the First Nations.

A similar optimism shines through another large piece entitled, *Circle of Concern.* This painting was inspired by a friend who was recovering from a serious car accident, according to David. Again, he addresses the dormancy of Native culture and the necessity of reviving it.

In *Circle of Concern,* he offers a path for the younger generation to follow. He shows that children possess all the hope and faith necessary to save the world.

David has reserved centre stage for the tree of life in a beautiful field. Unfortunately, the tree is half-dead, decayed at its core. It exists in a seemingly pleasant and nurturing habitat, but upon closer inspection the viewer can see an unhealthy environment all around. The bad air quality and the polluted ground water have deprived the tree of sustenance. The life force is poisoned by unseen forces.

At first glance, the forecast might appear bleak, but David leaves a treasure trove of strengthening images by including the bear, the turtle and the eagle as promises of salvation. At the bottom of the painting, he has placed the seven feathers representing the Seven Grandfather teachings. He has also etched the sacred mountains all around the circle; these are mountains that can only be seen by children.

"This is my brightest, most powerful painting," David said, indicating the twelve races of people visible in the circle of children. "Children are our hope for the future. They can re-learn the culture. They are the pipe carriers, the drummers, the doctors, the scientists. I see hope in the youth; I hope for strong youth to carry on."

For David, *Circle of Concern* represents a call for unity, understanding and healing. Since adults are sometimes too disillusioned by life experience, he believes children hold the key to saving the planet. Chances are, children haven't been tainted by negative influences and toxic ideas, so they can see a positive future.

"As we age, we tend to get cynical," he concluded. "But kids are hopeful and haven't lost faith."

And so it is with David. He is no longer the lost child of the *Woodland Nightmare*. Instead, he has survived with soul and mind intact to become an eclectic and courageous artist as well as an insightful and empathic human being.

His courage and willingness to try new things is apparent in all of his exhibitions. For example, his rendition of a bright California beach is somewhat startling juxtaposed with *Woodland Nightmare*. But, as he explains, the abrupt switch in mood and colour scheme is meant to give both the artist and the spectator more upbeat imagery.

"This *Looking for Gidget*, piece was all done through the imagination," he revealed. "It was something I needed to do; I wanted a break this past winter. I was wishing for warmer climes so I travelled in my imagination to California. Somehow the vision of masses of people on a California beach helped me to get out of that dark mood."

He often conjures up pleasant memories from childhood outings as a way to accentuate the positive. As he gazes upon a view of the North Channel towards M'Chigeeng Bay, he waxes nostalgic. Looking back he can almost smell the bannock and fish cooking on the shores of Eagle Island.

"We would go boating and fishing on the channel," he said. "There was some nice bass and pike fishing then. And we picked blueberries on Clapperton Island. Sometimes we just lived out there in the bush and slept overnight in a tent. There would be different families camping out there."

Memories of his mother and mentor are precious too. One of the most poignant paintings he has ever displayed is a portrait of the two of them standing together. It is entitled simply, *Mom and Me* and strongly conveys the abiding affection and respect of the mother/son duo. He pays homage to her as mother, artist and sustaining presence. Her guiding spirit is never very far from his side.

"She's around me once in a while whenever I smudge or pray or accomplish something particularly good," he said.

David also experiments in other artistic media to renew his inspiration or jumpstart his imagination. He credits another cousin, John Laford of Sault Ste. Marie, with sparking his interest in wood carving. At first he tried small two and four foot totem poles but later he graduated to more challenging and elaborate ones.

Antler carving is another favourite pastime. When Steve Radulovich Sr. gave him a set of moose antlers, David carved a touching and amusing scene of three bear figures and used a walnut stain to preserve the images. Although the *Bear Family* interaction is open to viewer interpretation, it appears as if one little bear wants to follow the Elder bear, but another little bear is trying to lead him astray.

David's work is prominently displayed at the Royal Ontario Museum, First Nations Collection, at the Whetung Art Gallery in Curve Lake, Ontario, at the McCord Museum, in Montreal and at the Ojibwe Cultural Foundation on Manitoulin Island. In addition, he had an exhibit at the Gore Bay Museum and Heritage Centre and participated in a group show at the Sheguiandah Centennial Museum.

During the summer of 2008, David organized the "Misquabigon Naaganuk" red clay pottery workshops, on Manitoulin. Students of all ages had a chance to experiment with ceramics under his patient tutelage. He invited people of all skill levels to come to his M'Chigeeng studio and try their hand at pots, bowls and sculptures. The biggest drawing card was the outdoor kiln he built from scratch.

Despite receiving widespread recognition and praise, he retains a modest and humble demeanor as he goes about his calling. He is a versatile artist who uses a variety of media to transform life experiences into messages of hope and redemption.

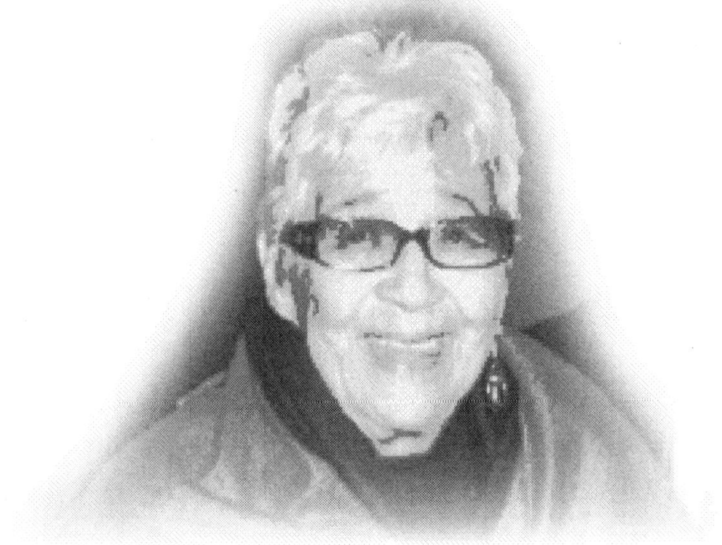

DAPHNE ODJIG (1919 -): Grandmother of the Manitoulin School

CHAPTER 11

Some people call her the Queen of Canadian Aboriginal Art; others refer to her as the First Lady of the Woodland School. Various regal titles have been bestowed upon Daphne Odjig over the years, in an effort to convey the respect and reverence felt by family, friends and admirers across the country. But in her home community of Wikwemikong, she is known simply as the Grandmother of the Manitoulin School of Art.

Although Daphne has been showered with tributes and accolades in recent years, the gatekeepers of the Canadian art establishment have not always been receptive to her work or her point of view. Throughout her career, she has been extremely versatile, creating a wide range of works including book illustrations, murals, mixed media canvases and abstract acrylics. It has taken a lifetime of grassroots activism and personal initiative to motivate national gallery administrators and cultural critics to acknowledge her place in Canadian history.

In 2009, she became the first Aboriginal woman to have a solo exhibition at the National Gallery of Canada. Such a crowning achievement would not have been possible without decades of intense study and self-discipline.

Growing up on Manitoulin Island, Daphne had always been immersed in her Potawatomi heritage and art in one form or another, according to her biographers Beth Southcott and Rosamund Vanderburgh. Daphne shared the details of her formative years with the authors in a 1992 publication entitled *A Paintbrush in My Hand*. In the dedication to the book, Daphne paid tribute to her grandfather Jonas Odjig, a renowned stonemason who carved ornate tombstones in their home community of Wikwemikong. Some of her earliest memories are of her grandfather sketching houses, church scenes and vignettes of village life. Along with design concepts, she absorbed local legends and memorable tales.

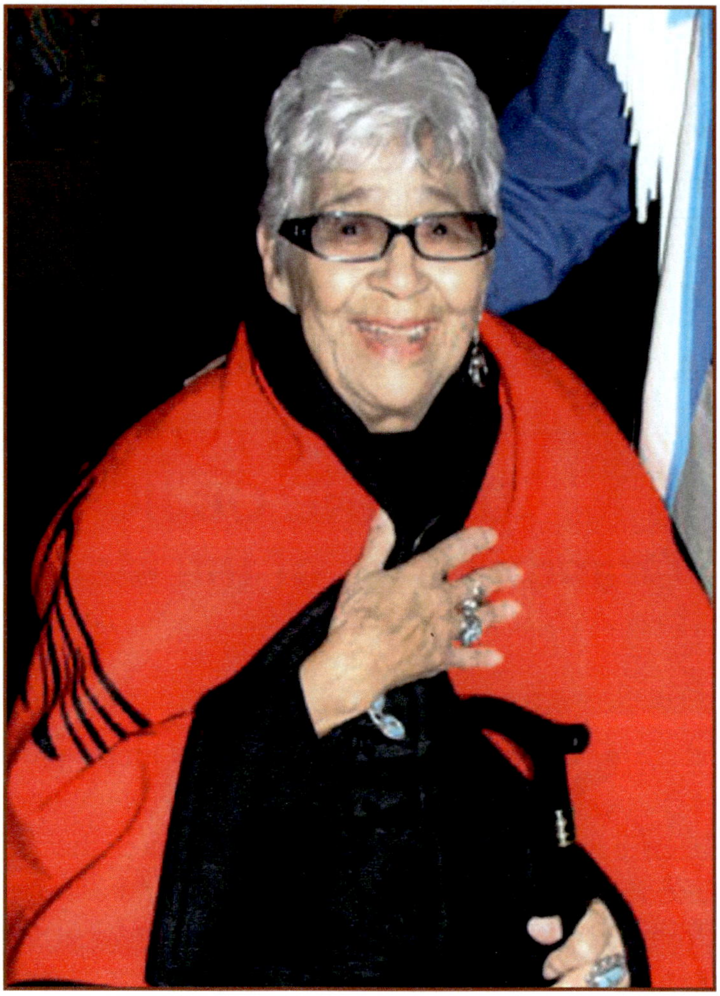

She also observed her veteran father, Dominic Odjig, painting portraits and scenes from his wartime experiences. Her mother, Joyce, an English war-bride, passed on her expertise with embroidery and knitting as well. As a youngster Daphne was nurtured by a creative extended family; however, it was a bout of rheumatic fever at age thirteen that forced Daphne into a lengthy period of convalescence where art became her pastime, and perhaps her personal salvation.

Southcott and Vanderburgh reported that Daphne lived a relatively cloistered life in Wikwemikong, an island community with a long history of independence and self-sufficiency. Educated in a Jesuit-run school until grade seven, she loved to draw and explore the nuances of watercolours. Even as a child, she was described as a hard worker who was adept at picking up skills through observation and emulation.

The security of a loving and protective environment came to an end when Daphne was eighteen. Her mother passed away in 1938, followed shortly thereafter by her grandfather. *A Paintbrush in My Hand* also documented the realities of racism and discrimination she and her siblings faced when they were removed from their childhood home by their maternal grandmother. In order to find employment in her new circumstances, Daphne changed her name to Fisher for a time and survived by waiting on tables in Parry Sound. In those difficult years, it was common for First Nations people in urban centres to camouflage their identity in order to navigate mainstream society. Undoubtedly, the demands of earning a living left little time for her art, but she continued to sketch and create Christmas cards and decorative jewellery boxes.

As a young woman, she moved to Toronto where she found factory work during World War Two. As she explored the art galleries of the city, she satisfied her hunger to learn more about art traditions such as Cubism, Expressionism and Abstract styles. She studied European painters such as Rembrandt and Rubens, as well as Canadian works by Tom Thomson and the Group of Seven. Since she had been raised in a household that emphasized self-education, it was second nature for her to learn the techniques of the French Impressionists such as Renoir and Monet without a tutor.

Although the inner drive for artistic self-expression was ever present, she was also receptive to romance and travel. When she met Paul Somerville, a Mohawk/Metis veteran, and relocated to British Columbia to be married in August 1945, it signalled an interlude of happiness and contentment. Daphne enjoyed the companionship of a spouse who encouraged her art and pride in Native ancestry. During this phase, she was working in pencil, pastel, charcoal and oil. Like many artists during the 1950s, she was drawn to the innovations of Pablo Picasso and Cubism. As always, one of her greatest strengths was the ability to study other art forms and integrate elements she liked into her own evolving style.

Paul and Daphne carved out a life for themselves in the Fraser Valley of British Columbia and raised two sons. Tragically, all their plans for future projects were shattered in 1960 when Paul died from injuries received in a car accident.

After her husband's death, Daphne found solace in her art and devoted herself to developing her own unique icons and techniques. The 1960s would bring geographical and spiritual changes that were mirrored in her sketchpads and canvases.

In 1962 a new adventure began when she married Chester Beavon. During their honeymoon, they paid a visit to relatives in Wikwemikong before moving to Northern Manitoba, where her husband was a community development officer. His challenging task was to assist the Cree people displaced by massive dam projects infringing on their traditional fishing grounds. These postings at Grand Rapids and later at Easterville, would inspire Daphne to take her art in a dramatic direction. Previously, she had painted landscapes, and had sold some in Vancouver, but now she turned her acute powers of observation to human figures. It was her poignant pen-and-ink drawings of the Cree people left in limbo by hydro-electric developments, that sparked empathy in viewers. Her sensitive and accurate portrayals of the hopelessness and desolation of dislocation, struck a chord with art buyers in Winnipeg and elsewhere.

Although Daphne continued to be stimulated and intrigued by the terrain of British Columbia and Manitoba, her thoughts were never very far from Northern Ontario. On Manitoulin Island she had inherited an artistic sensibility and a rich oral tradition that would form the foundation of much of her work. At pivotal points in her life, she made momentous pilgrimages back to her Wikwemikong roots.

One of the most life-altering journeys home came in 1964, when Daphne was forty-five. In this turbulent era, the Red Power and civil rights movements were gaining momentum throughout Turtle Island and Manitoulin residents were not isolated from this continental shift in consciousness. Artist and curator Bonnie Devine has highlighted this important transition in her mentor's career in a 2007 essay entitled, "From Resistance to Renewal." In the catalogue accompanying the landmark, "Odjig Retrospective Exhibition," at the Art Gallery of Sudbury, she suggested that the events of that summer reunion had a profound impact on Daphne's outlook.

First Nations cultural practices had been banned from 1884 until 1951, Devine pointed out in her essay. But in the 1960s, the ceremonies that had been driven underground were resurfacing and Wikwemikong was in the forefront of this cultural revival. When Daphne went home for her community's fourth annual pow wow, she was reunited with many former acquaintances involved in rediscovering repressed rituals. One of the key players was her sister-in-law, Rosemary Peltier, a prime mover behind reinstating the traditional gathering. On this occasion, she presented Daphne with a women's ceremonial dress and invited her to join the pow wow dancers. In interviews with Ms. Devine, Daphne remembered that the sights and the sounds of that day's celebration moved her to fully embrace her heritage.

Perhaps a work entitled, *Pow Wow Dancer* (1978), best exemplifies the energizing spirit of her initial pow wow experiences. The acrylic on canvas painting vibrates with banners of brilliant colour as the exuberant dancer, entranced by the drumming, emerges from a swirling circle of reds, blues, greens. In full regalia, the dancer appears buoyant, challenging the boundaries of the circle, feet barely touching the ground.

For Daphne, this surge of energy and confidence was only the beginning of an on-going spiritual awakening. Through Rosemary Peltier, Daphne was re-introduced to many of the keepers of traditional knowledge in Wikwemikong. As she had been in childhood, Daphne was once again immersed in the legends and creation stories of her youth.

As it turned out, the exciting developments in Wikwemikong would boost the careers of many First Nations artists, according to Devine. The pow wows attracted then Prime Minister Lester B. Pearson, also the MP for Algoma-Manitoulin. His interest and support would prove to be fortuitous. He purchased over a hundred works on display at a local First Nations art show organized by Daphne and Tom Peltier Jr. In this manner, the national Aboriginal art collection was started at the Department of Indian and Northern Affairs (DINA) in Ottawa.

The joy of preserving oral history was brought home in interactions with the Wikwemikong elders. Throughout the late 1960s and early 1970s, Daphne would reconnect with the lore that Jonas and other storytellers had shared with her. Her appreciation of this legacy was expressed in the tender portrait she created of *Aunt Grace and the Elders* (1978). In this acrylic on canvas work, the storytellers are depicted in a close-knit circle of unity and mutual support as they pass their wisdom to the next generation.

Daphne accepted responsibility for aiding in the transmission of the stories. In the 1970s, many Manitoulin Island school children were able to follow the antics of Nanabozho, the trickster, in ten booklets of illustrated legends she created for the Ojibwe Cultural Foundation. For years afterwards, when she appeared in public, former students would approach her for autographs, clutching well-thumbed copies of their old readers in their hands. Clearly they treasured the oft-told stories such as *Nanabush and the Dancing Ducks* and *Nanabush and the Spirit of Winter*.

Although she lived and painted internationally in the old world historic sites of Yugoslavia, Sweden and Israel, she always maintained a connection with her own Manitoulin history. Works such as the nostalgic piece entitled, *Playing School* (1981), evoke memories of her elementary school years in Wikwemikong. In this intimate scene she has painted the forms of the teacher and the attentive students in earth tones. The trusting eyes of the children are cast upward in expectation and respect. Another piece in the island memories series recreates carefree outings to the lake near her childhood home. In *The Old Swimming Hole* (1981), the children are laughing, diving, splashing with the total abandon so characteristic of that age of innocence. Again the figures are rendered in soft, sandy or chocolate browns.

Even when she was thousands of miles from Manitoulin, Daphne could reach back in memory and conjure up the simple pleasures that characterized her early upbringing. She found ways to keep in touch with her birthplace through her art and occasional trips back to Manitoulin. She was particularly supportive of the Ojibwe Cultural Foundation, a M'Chigeeng-based centre devoted to the preservation of First Nations language and culture. Prints of her painting, *The Dreamcatcher*, were used as a fund-raising tool for the centre's capital building fund. Ironically, the OCF's new facilities unveiled in 1999 were deemed inadequate to host a major retrospective of her work that travelled throughout the country 2008 to 2009.

In childhood, Daphne had dreamed of becoming a teacher and had spent many hours conducting play school, according to her biographers. Therefore, it was fitting that she be invited to teach at Tom Peltier's Manitou Arts Foundation in 1971. Accompanied by artist Carl Ray and poet Duke Redbird, she joined aspiring young artists such as Martin Panamick, Leland Bell, Blake Debassige, Randy C. Trudeau and Shirley Cheechoo at Schreiber Island, an oasis for creativity in Georgian Bay. With the summer art camp participants, her instruction was informal but appealing to her young charges. She would paint alongside the teens, modelling her own techniques and then her proteges would have leisure to master and modify the skills through personal experimentation. This unpressured environment allowed the novices to develop at their own pace. Clearly, it was important for Daphne not to impose her own values and perceptions on the emerging talent. And to this day the Schreiber Island alumni express appreciation for this respectful philosophy.

The sojourn at Schreiber Island also gave Daphne an opportunity to learn more about her Potawatomi heritage and led her to a deepening appreciation for her grandfather and other ancestors. In interviews with Vanderburgh and Southcott, Daphne shared stories of her great-great-grandfather, the compassionate and heroic Chief Black Partridge. His recurring image appears throughout her body of work.

Despite her low-key approach, Daphne would be regarded as a trailblazer during a period when First Nations people continued to encounter widespread discrimination and disrespect. Barred from mainstream galleries, she worked quietly, but persistently, to bring Aboriginal art out of the dark corners of Canadian museums. As she made inroads herself, she consciously took time out from her own work to assist other First Nations artists.

In her youth, she had struggled to build self-confidence and to clarify her individual artistic style. In mid-life, however, she reached a threshold where she no longer had misgivings about asserting herself and breaking new ground. In 1972, she unleashed her boundless vision to create a mural entitled, *The Creation of the World*, at the Manitoba Museum of Man. And her progressive spirit was the impetus for a seminal show at the Winnipeg Art Gallery in 1972. With the "Treaty Numbers 23, 287 and 1171" exhibition, another milestone was reached. It was the first time Native artists had been featured in a Canadian public art gallery rather than a museum.

The founding of the Professional Native Indian Artists' Association, in 1973, was further evidence of her courage and foresight. The group later dubbed, "The Indian Group of Seven," included Daphne, Carl Ray, Jackson Beardy, Joseph Sanchez, Eddy Cobiness, Norval Morrisseau and Alex Janvier.

Alex Janvier, one of the outspoken members of the original group, holds bittersweet memories of those volatile times and the colourful characters who worked to shake up the status quo.

"We started this vision in the early 70s," he told a Laurentian University audience in 2007. "We got together at Daphne's place in Winnipeg. She was a very special, very strong woman. She was like a mother to the rest of us fools."

With so many creative minds in one group, it seemed inevitable that personality clashes and differences of opinion would occur. With his trademark wit and no-holds-barred style, Janvier credits Daphne with steering the often unwieldy group in a positive direction.

"We were crazy," he said. "Some of us had some pretty crazy ideas. Sometimes we'd get in fights; sometimes the Haida would pick on the Anishinaabe. Some of us were educated in regular school and some of us were educated in the school of hard knocks. Carl Ray is gone now, but he was full of mischief. Jackson Beardy was a real playboy with the ladies. But Eddy Cobiness was a traditional man with straight answers. He always got right to the point. And Morrisseau, well he wanted to go to Russia and do a show, but the Cold War was on then so it didn't happen."

Despite the apparent conflicts and the sometimes haphazard approach to the stumbling blocks facing First Nations artists, the collective under Daphne's leadership battered away at the persistent barriers.

"At that time there were a lot of closed doors; we (First Nations artists) were shoved into the museums and the government funded galleries wouldn't even look at us," Janvier said. "There were journalists who snickered behind our backs and compared us to the Canadian Group of Seven, but we had a different view. We had a vision so we just pushed ahead. Eventually, we ripped apart the apartheid of Canadian art."

Of course, it was a slow process to convince mainstream galleries to open up their doors. For the most part First Nations artists were blocked from Canadian art institutions. But as members of the collective, such as Morrisseau, earned wider acceptance and exposure, more opportunities arose for the others.

"One by one the galleries fell in love with us," Janvier said. "Some of us became moderately successful. And after that the painting started to speak for us and we didn't have to defend ourselves. But remember, none of us got a bloody grant or even a plug nickel all those years. We had to scrounge to travel back and forth. We have been tested in every way, but we are a strong people and we have survived. We all went on to develop our own styles."

One of Janvier's colleagues, Joseph Sanchez is equally grateful for the work of Daphne with the Professional Native Indian Artists' Association (later incorporated as Professional Native Artists, Inc.) He was novice painter, barely out of his teens, when he became part of the Indian Group of Seven in Winnipeg in 1974. Later he returned home to the United States to serve as curator with the Institute of American Indian Arts in Santa Fe, New Mexico. During a symposium on the Woodland School in 2007, he praised her for the help she has given to Native artists in both practical and spiritual matters.

"Daphne bought people's art and gave people opportunities to show their art," he told the gathering at Laurentian University. "Daphne's energy guided us. With her, it was always about the art. At that time, there was not much funding for Native arts and our art was often relegated to souvenir shops and craft stores. Many artists made less than $1000 a year then."

In his address to the Sudbury audience, Sanchez reiterated his enduring respect for Daphne.

"I was just twenty, then, so I learned a lot of lessons from the other artists," he noted. "I was just barely learning how to paint, so I was amazed to be part of this group. I felt welcomed and it gave me strength and courage to speak out. I also enjoyed many late night conversations with Daphne on those cold Winnipeg winters. And I spent a very productive time drawing in her studio. She was a mentor and a friend; she helped Indian artists both emotionally and financially."

When he returned to the American Southwest and progressed in his own career, her encouraging words and her activist spirit sustained him. And the lines, the energy and the movement of Daphne's paintings stayed with him when he went on to forge his own style. After the stint in Canada, he worked to change entrenched perceptions in his home territory of New Mexico and Arizona.

Daphne's generosity and philosophy of life have had a lasting impact on Sanchez and his current work.

"My life was formed up here," he said. "These were very exciting times for me. I was young and inexperienced and I was embraced by some of Canada's greatest artists. A lot of the ideas that I took home with me came out of that early group of seven. It taught me that glory and success are not important. Helping our indigenous people is what is important."

In his view, Daphne and the collective played an invaluable role at a time when mainstream society treated contemporary Native art as a cultural artifact.

"I believe it helped to force the galleries to accept Native artists," he concluded. "It allowed artists to show in galleries they could only dream about before. Our cause was simple: to exhibit our work and to be accepted as Native artists."

In their testaments, Janvier and Sanchez illustrated how Daphne endeared herself to fellow artists by working to ensure that they could weather the lean times. In 1974 her Winnipeg shop expanded to become the New Warehouse Gallery, a bold step in her campaign to support emerging Native artists. It was more than a showcase for neglected talent; it was a magnet for people who recognized the need for a communal approach to solving problems. As the owner and operator of the first Native owned print shop and gallery in Canada, she was paving the way for future generations of First Nations entrepreneurs.

Lake Shuswap, in the Okanagan Valley of British Columbia, became her personal home base in 1976. But before long, Manitoulin became the centre of the art universe again. The first National Native Artists' Conference was held at M'Chigeeng First Nation from October 23-25, 1978. Predictably, Daphne was a guiding force in another history-making event. The national gathering gave her a welcome chance to stay on home turf in Wikwemikong, where a feast was held in her honour and she enjoyed reminiscing with relatives. In addition, her home community presented her with an eagle feather in recognition of her courageous work on behalf of First Nations.

Speakers such as Alex Janvier, Carl Beam, Tom Hill, Doreen Jansen, David General, Bob Boyer and Tony Hunt travelled to Manitoulin to add their voices to the forum. The aim of the national gathering, according to The Native Perspective magazine (Vol 3, #2, 1978), was to bring Indian artists from across Canada to share their experiences, frustrations, insights and resources. Mentors such as Daphne and renowned Haida artist, Bill Reid, briefed emerging artists on how to take control of their careers.

This conference was followed by a similar one in K'san British Columbia in 1983.

Collaborating with other artists and simultaneously clarifying her own perspectives would eventually pay off and some important commissions came her way. For instance, in 1978, she unveiled *The Indian in Transition*, a four part mural commissioned for the national Museum of Man. The following year she was invited by the McMichael Canadian Collection in Kleinburg, Ontario to complete the monumental *Rebirth of a Culture*. And in 1984, Sudbury's Laurentian University also called upon her to paint a piece entitled, *Spiritual Renewal*, for their museum and art centre.

Back home on Manitoulin Island, people were working behind the scenes to identify other ways to permanently commemorate her contributions to community, province and nation. At the prodding of Tom Peltier Jr., the Ontario Geographic Names Board agreed to name an island and a reef off the east shore of Wikwemikong in honour of Daphne and her late confidante and sister-in-law, Rosemary Fisher Odjig. In August 2007, Squaw Island and Squaw Island Bank were designated Odjig Island and Odjig Island Bank, with the blessings of Wikwemikong and the town of Northeastern Manitoulin and the Islands.

In his petition for the name change, Peltier had stressed the key role played by both women in the cultural and artistic renaissance ignited in Wikwemikong during the 1960s.

The geographic tribute in summer, 2007, was followed by another emotional event that autumn as Daphne enjoyed a triumphant homecoming to Northern Ontario. The Art Gallery of Sudbury hosted a retrospective of her work organized by artist and curator, Bonnie Devine. The landmark exhibit was held in conjunction with "Witness, a Symposium on the Woodland School," held at Laurentian University, October 12-14. She travelled from her adopted Penticton home to bask in the warmth of universal affection displayed by old friends and new fans alike.

For Bonnie Devine, the curator of the Sudbury exhibit and conference, the event promised to be a groundbreaking occasion. Ontario residents had not seen a significant collection of Daphne's work since 1985 when a retrospective had been mounted by the Thunder Bay Art Gallery.

"This retrospective of this great Canadian artist is long overdue," Devine said during the opening ceremonies. "This exhibit is very significant for this region so it was important to have the retrospective as close as possible to Daphne's birthplace."

As Daphne, the guest of honour, toured the Sudbury gallery, she complimented the curator on the design of the showcase. She was pleased to see all of her works from the past four decades arranged decade by decade to demonstrate the breadth of her exploration and experimentation.

"I am very honoured," she said. "They did a marvellous job of hanging the paintings. It was very emotional and very touching."

Surrounded by friends and relations from Wikwemikong, she paused to reflect on a life journey that has taken her from Manitoulin Island to Manitoba, to the West Coast and across the seas.

"It feels wonderful to be home," she said. "I have met lots of people, some I haven't seen for years. And I have met lots of people I used to go to school with, so there are many familiar faces on this visit."

However, she did express regret that many of her old friends have passed on to the spirit world.

"I am so grateful that I lived this long to witness it all. And I know all the artists who have passed on are with me in spirit."

One of the highlights of the Laurentian University event, was an original dramatic production by Debajehmujig Theatre Group of Wikwemikong. The innovative troupe performed a heartwarming play called, *Dear Daphne*, a piece designed to demonstrate the richness of her legacy and to reinforce her message to the world.

"I am very honoured," she said after the presentation. "I am just overwhelmed. I never expected anything like this. There are no words for it. I just loved the little Daphne in the play. Miigwetch to you all."

When asked to offer a few words of advice for today's aspiring artists, Daphne spoke without hesitation. "Get a good education," she said. "Art comes from your heart and your spirit, so if you feel artistically inclined, follow that path."

Daphne was increasingly in the spotlight during 2008. The Canadian Museum of Civilization located in Gatineau, Quebec, hosted a collection of her serigraphs on paper entitled, "Daphne Odjig: Four Decades of Prints". The show included *The Jerusalem Series*, commissioned by El Al Airlines (1975-76), as well as, *Tales From the Smokehouse*, a series of erotica completed for author Herbert T. Schwarz (1974).

During her prestigious career, Daphne has been the recipient of many honours. In June 2008, an honourary Doctor of Laws degree, was bestowed upon her in ceremonies at Western University, London, Ontario. Recognition came in 2007, as well, when she accepted the "Governor General's Award," in visual and media arts. "The Xpression Award," an initiative of the National Film Board of Canada in 2003, served as recognition of Daphne as a champion of cultural diversity. Okanagan University College celebrated her achievements in 2002 with an honourary Doctor of Letters. A "National Aboriginal Achievement Award," was presented to her in 1998. In addition, she has been a member of "The Order of Canada," since 1986. Northern Ontario universities Laurentian (1982) and Nipissing (1986) have expressed appreciation to the North's favourite daughter with honourary degrees as well.

During all the ceremonies and tributes, Daphne has accepted the praise with humility, modesty and dignity. As the undisputed Queen of the Woodland School and Grandmother of the Manitoulin School, she has nurtured generations of aspiring First Nations artists.

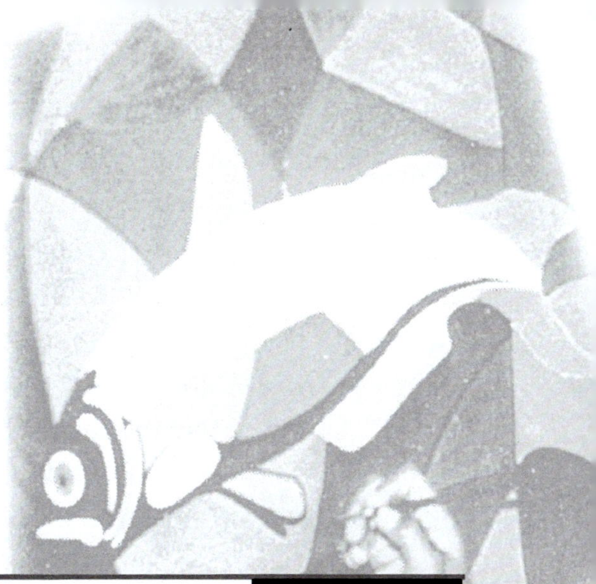

CHAPTER 12

A posthumous tribute to MARTIN PANAMICK (1954 - 1977)

During the preparation of this series of Manitoulin artist profiles, the legacy of the late Martin Panamick was frequently mentioned by his fellow artists. Although he perished in a tragic traffic accident during the summer of 1977, his memory lives on in his family's art tradition and in the limited collection of his works at the Ojibwe Cultural Foundation (OCF) and elsewhere.

In order to compose a posthumous tribute, I met with Martin's sister Patricia Panamick and their first cousin, Kate Roy, to discuss Martin's contributions to the Manitoulin School of Art.

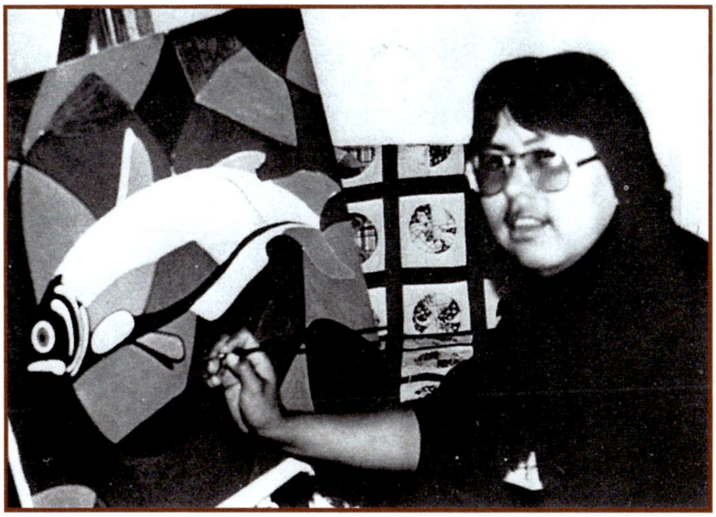

Born in 1954, Martin was the eldest of eight children, and an influential role model for the younger generation. His siblings included Marjorie, Roy, Stanley, Patricia, Lydia, Bill and Alice (predeceased.) Although she was only eleven when she lost her big brother, Patricia Panamick has inherited her family's appreciation of the OCF and its dedication to preserving the Ojibwe language and to supporting First Nations.

"When I was a little girl, I would see Martin painting on an easel," she recalled. "He lived for his artwork; it was his passion. From morning to night he loved to paint."

From the age of twelve, Patricia witnessed the creativity of her family role models, so it seemed perfectly normal to follow in their footsteps. Over the years, she has continued her beadwork and leatherwork and has won several design competitions including the logos for M'Chigeeng's Lakeview School and The Two Bears Cultural Survival Group. In addition, visitors to M'Chigeeng can see her handiwork on a billboard at the entrance to the community. In 2007, she took on a labour of love for the OCF. In her capable hands, a Thunderbird logo, originally designed by Martin for OCF hasty notes and stationery, was reproduced on deer hide and given new life. The work currently holds a prominent place in the OCF gallery and stands as an enduring testament to Panamick creativity.

"Doing art just takes your mind off things," she confided. "I have worked as an instructor at the OCF and I have also worked in the schools. In a way, I am carrying on my Mom's good works (Theresa Panamick passed away in 1997). I am also finishing my grade 12 so that I can teach more workshops in the future."

Patricia has made herself invaluable at the OCF in more ways than one. She is known far and wide as a fine cook and creator of some very tasty and sought-after scone.

But on the day of our interview, in January 2009, she was in a solemn and reflective mood. Memories came flooding back as she opened a well-preserved artist's sketch pad that had belonged to her brother. As she turned the pages of the treasured notebook, featuring Martin's drawings made thirty years ago, she paused to meditate on things that might have been. Had he lived to see the new millennium, Martin would most certainly have been a grandfather now, she said. And as she revisited the images of the sea serpent, the bear and the thunderbird in her bother's personal notebook, she expressed confidence that he would have been a world renowned artist if death hadn't claimed him prematurely.

"I named my son Martin after my oldest brother," she added. "I was about eleven when he passed on to the spirit world, so I never really got to know him, but he set a good example for me. Today everyone still talks about him with admiration."

Kate Roy, cultural services liaison and a mainstay at the OCF since the 1970s, also speaks of Martin with great affection and regard.

"When I came to the OCF to work, it was a time when our language and culture were coming to the surface once again," she recalled. "Since our culture was in a period of revitalization, I saw many artists at the OCF including Randy Trudeau, Don Ense, Blake Debassige, Blair Debassige, James Simon, Leland Bell and, of course, Martin."

His mother, Theresa Panamick, was a tremendous influence on the young artist, according to Kate. In the mid-70s, the family matriarch was passing on cultural teachings and her excellent beadwork skills to youth at the OCF.

As Martin was immersed in the local and national cultural renewal, he was moved to depict Ojibwe legends in acrylic and watercolour. He possessed an innate sense about what was appropriate to share in his art.

"He was such a quiet guy, but at the same time very sensitive to his work and to making sure he didn't put anything on paper that he shouldn't," Kate said.

As artist in residence at the OCF, Martin was commissioned to illustrate a line of notepaper as well as calendars and limited edition serigraphs. Books such as *Ko-Ko-Ko The Owl*, *Why the Beaver has a Broad Tail* and *Nishnabe Delights*, featured his memorable motifs. During his tenure at OCF, he participated in several group exhibitions including one at Laurentian University, in Sudbury. His work was last exhibited overseas November 8-18, 1977 at the Marcon IV in Rome, Italy.

Although Martin's artwork is a rare find now, the OCF still has some of his original paintings in their permanent collection as well as three of his paintings on deer hide. His work can still be found in public spaces such as the Immaculate Conception Church, Lakeview School and band council chambers in M'Chigeeng. The Royal Ontario Museum, the McMichael Canadian Collection, Woodland Studios (Cutler, Ontario) and Lillian's Museum in M'Chigeeng, all treasure Martin's work in their permanent collections.

According to *Anishnabe Mee-Kun*, a catalogue published by the OCF in 1984, Martin was an important early member of the Manitoulin School of Art and his enthusiasm encouraged many of his contemporaries to paint, particularly his younger brother Stanley.

M.E. Southcott, author of *Sound of the Drum*, noted that Martin was primarily a "self-taught" artist, although he did attend the summer arts program offered by Tom Peltier's Manitou Arts Foundation in 1972. He was also a member of the "Indian Art Club" at Manitoulin Secondary School. Southcott describes Martin's style as "graceful yet economical," revealing a strong attraction to the motifs found on ancient birch bark scrolls. As his career was taking off, he was experimenting with Cubism and other European art traditions as well.

In an interview with Southcott, Theresa Panamick described her son as "a teacher and protector" to his younger siblings and she characterized him as generally "fun-loving and sociable."

Patricia and Kate also remembered Martin as a free spirit who loved to don his helmet and jacket and take off on his motorcycle.

"Artwork was his passion," they said. "But along the way he bought himself a Honda bike. Whenever he felt the urge for a break from the work, he would fly away."

Unfortunately, the bike that was his symbol of freedom, would ultimately take his life at age twenty-three. A collision with a school bus in the summer of 1977, cut short his promising art career and left his family and admirers in mourning.

Today the Panamick family carries on the artistic tradition celebrated by Martin. His brother, Stanley, is gaining a reputation with his traditional Woodland style paintings. His nephew, the young Martin Panamick, is evolving into a talented writer and artist and another nephew, Peter Panamick, is drawing praise for his beautiful and realistic sketches of animals. As for sister Patricia, she continues to paint and to refine the exquisite craft making skills she learned from her mother. Of course, it's not just her art that complements events at the OCF. She still makes the delicious, mouth-watering scone that keeps visitors coming back for more.

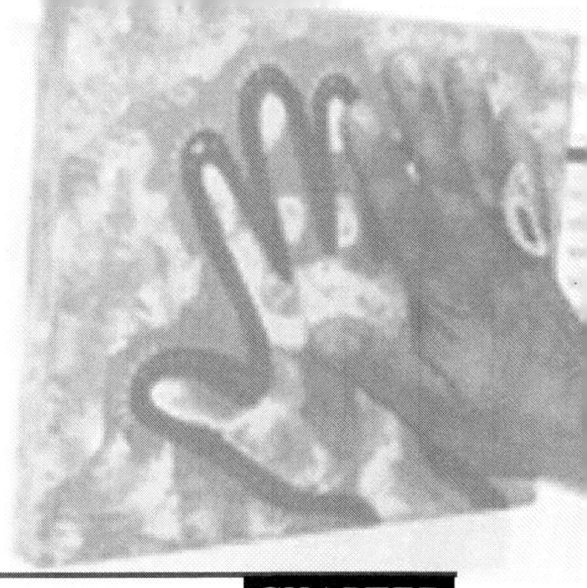

CHAPTER 13

MARY PHEASANT (1955 -): Dancing on Canvas

Making art is a mystical process that cannot be forced or fabricated. And when an artist has something important to say, the urgency to express it is often overwhelming. For many individuals, the impulse to create cannot be suppressed or denied.

Odawa artist Mary Maaniinhs Pheasant, always knew deep down inside of herself that she was an artist. However, for several decades, life circumstances and psychological barriers prevented her from following her instincts. Fortunately, for the art world, Mary has surmounted some of the obstacles impeding her progress and has entered a period of prolific output.

This emerging artist was born on the Wikwemikong Unceded Indian Reserve in 1955. As a child, she and some of her seven brothers would spend many evenings around the handmade kitchen table drawing on scraps of paper. In fact, they would draw on anything they could find, including the walls, much to their mother's dismay. Although resources were sometimes scarce, education, music and art were always emphasized in her family. Mary's father, Alexander Jacko, a self-taught musician, painted acrylic murals in their home and taught himself to become an electronics technician, among other things. Her mother, Blanche, who also had a talent for singing and playing the organ, expressed her creativity and cultural pride in a variety of handicrafts including beadwork and Native dance regalia. Oral history also played a significant role in stimulating her imagination. By listening to Elders' stories, Mary was immersed in both her community and world history.

"When we were small we had no television," she recalled. "We would listen to the radio, which was turned on from morning till night. And from a very early age we would read. Books and paper were always immensely treasured by all of us back then as they still are today. Actually, when we didn't have books, it was as if we were starving for them. In my family, I learned that I could do anything I put my mind to."

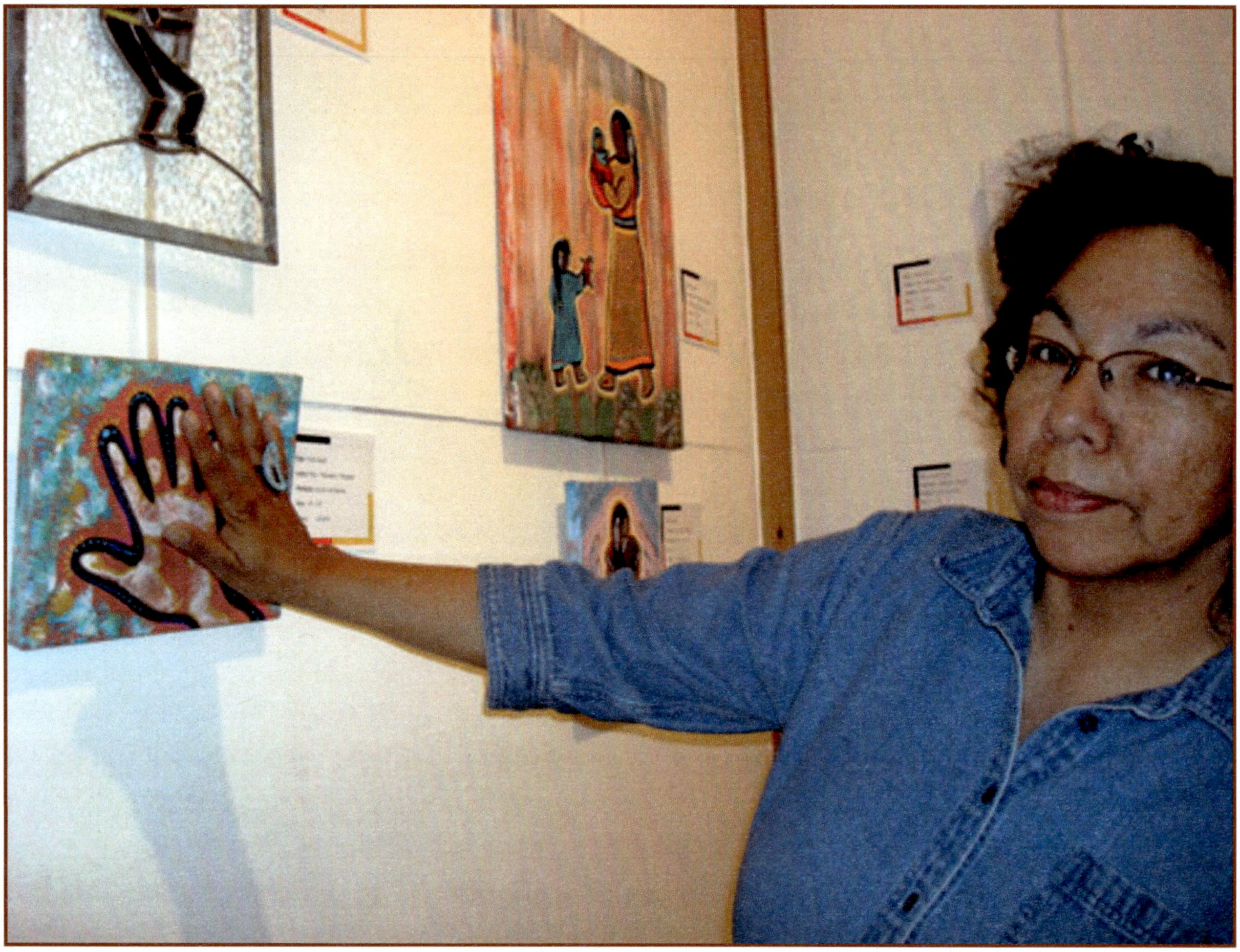

With these positive role models to inspire her, Mary always set high goals for herself. She married her "best friend," Robert Pheasant, and went on to receive her Bachelor of Arts in Humanities from Laurentian University in Western Philosophy and Native Studies. In addition, she graduated from the Cambrian College diabetes education and care program. She was proud to become the first certified Native Nutrition Manager in Canada. But during all the years of raising her son and daughter and caring for her clients, she was nurturing another dream as well.

In June 2005, she picked up the paintbrush she had discarded during a troubled passage in her youth. At age nineteen she had abandoned her artwork in reaction to family grief and trauma. It would be thirty years before she had the courage to revisit her childhood memories. Slowly, under the tutelage of her brother James Jacko, her life experiences were revealed in acrylic and canvas. With the help of her son Luke, owner of Fezent Digital Media Productionz, she distributed some of her images on note cards. The miniatures were well-received by visitors to Artists on Elgin, in Sudbury and Manitoulin's Ojibwe Cultural Foundation in M'Chigeeng.

"I started making the cards because I want everyone to have a piece of the art," she explained.

In her work she articulates the importance of love, generosity and sharing. Themes of inter-generational connection and family bonding also predominate. Her vibrant canvases frequently celebrate the bounties of Nature as well.

She is particularly fond of her first painting, entitled, *My Brothers* (2005), based on a recollection of June strawberry picking expeditions with her siblings. The work was completed three years ago when she was recuperating from a painful bout with shingles. At that time, she was just beginning to heed the insistence of her inner voice and to allow the past to resurface.

"I had to become very ill physically, before I listened to the Creator and allowed myself to accept this blessing that I was given," she said.

Her relationship with her brother sustained her while she continued to experiment and grow in confidence.

"My younger brother had always encouraged me to enter this realm," she added. "He has been a fantastic guide and mentor."

As she delved deeper into her cultural legacy, images such as *Mshkiki* emerged. In this portrait, a slight figure in reddish brown garments holds an eagle feather fan with turtle symbol in one hand and a drum in the other. Eagle spirit lines pierce the pink and blue background. This design was destined to be reproduced by her husband Robert in one of his stained glass creations.

"I was still learning at this point," she said. "My brother was helping me. I was advancing quickly and he would urge me to just keep it up. When I finally knew what I wanted to paint, it just came out. I did not realize that I was developing my own style. It was other artists such as Ben Hinmon-Kingfisher and Francis Kagige as well as curators at Bear Claw Gallery in Edmonton and Ziibiwiing Cultural Centre in Mount Pleasant who recognized this. My brothers James and Marcel also told me that I was so fortunate to have developed my own style so early on in my art career. They encouraged me to keep on painting no matter what."

Embarking on an entirely new career can be daunting, but Mary was determined to break down her own personal barriers which held her back. After all, overcoming barriers has always been a family tradition.

Meeting with other artists, such as Natasha Smoke Santiago, Michael Roanhorse, Ray "Tainoray" Riviera, Jerry Laktonen and Shane Hendron during the Smithsonian Holiday Art Market also provided much encouragement and artistic advice for her.

"What can I paint?," she asked herself. "I was so afraid of failing. I knew that I could not paint like anyone else did. I could paint only the way that I could."

Although she didn't feel qualified at first, she gradually grew more comfortable with the label of artist. And soon she was taking bold steps to honestly portray the mixture of tears and joy that are part of everyone's life path. In her work as a diabetes educator, she often counselled clients in their efforts to lead a healthy life. This universal struggle to achieve balance is woven into her works of art.

"I paint what I know," she said. "It just comes; I let it come out. I had to learn how to break through my unseen walls in order to be free to 'dance' on the canvas."

Her rendition of *The Red Road*, for example, evokes many of these common themes. A red banner bearing traditional Ojibwe floral motifs loops from frame to frame illustrating the curves and dips so characteristic of the human journey. The imagery suggests that, although we all experience our share of sorrow, there are also moments of exquisite joy.

"In life there are barriers, there are deaths of loved ones to cope with," she confided. "But we learn to live with them. You don't ever get over them; they become part of who you are."

This spirit of acceptance is evident in a tribute to her mother who passed away in September 1994. In *Zhiitawin*, Mary has presented a figure clad in a bright orange dress; around her waist is a belt adorned with poppies. She is sitting at her dresser arranging a feather in her hair. The images are based on a dream sequence related by Robert Pheasant. In the vision, Mary's mother was telling them, "I'm getting ready to go." From her peaceful demeanor, one senses she is preparing to enter the spirit world.

The same respectful and affectionate approach is also apparent in *B'maadzawin* (My Life), which depicts a small figure leaning against a rock. His head is bent back and he gazes meditatively towards a luminous sky. For Mary, this image conveys the essence of her father's values and outlook on life.

Memories of her father also inspired *Green Apples*, a warm and sentimental look at a meaningful family custom. The painting recreates the close-knit relationship between parent and child as the father carries one child on his shoulders and another runs by his side. Even the family dog trots contentedly toward home. Along the way, they are all munching on green apples.

"My Dad worked as a custodian at what is now known as the Day Star Centre," Mary related. "Sometimes he took us with him as he went to do his job. And on the way home we would pick green apples and chokecherries. If I was tired, he would throw me on his shoulders and carry me. Sometimes I would wear Dad's hat."

A sense of strong family connection also shines through a piece entitled, *Nookomis*. It depicts a grandmother figure dressed in purple garments and wearing a blue kerchief on her head. She clutches her purse and holds the hand of a small child. The child, clad in a green and yellow dress, hurries to keep up with grandmother.

The theme of familial ties is also present in the colourful canvas she calls *Sharing*. The painting, inspired by the graduation of her cousin's daughter as a midwife, shows a mother holding a baby boy in a red bunting bag. Down below her is a small child holding up a little brown doll (also dressed in red to symbolize strength.)

Another of her heart-warming images is entitled, *Num Nums*. In the painting, a mother figure dressed in a blue dress and white apron hands out strawberries to the eagerly outstretched hand of a child. It harks back to a time when children anticipated the treats handed out by the adults at New Year celebrations.

Of all the themes in her work to date, love emerges as one of the most enduring. From her fourteen years experience as a palliative care provider, Mary has learned the importance of therapeutic touch. In giving comfort to elders in the last stages of their lives, she has observed the healing power of a simple hug.

In a piece entitled, *Life Hand*, she addresses both the happiness and grief inherent in the human passage from birth to death. She believes that despite the painful setbacks, despite the shattered dreams and lost hopes, there's still a powerful life force helping people persevere.

Mary reminds her audience that the government sanctioned, church run residential school system, deprived generations of First Nations children of parental love and guidance. Children were taught to suppress their emotions and hide their tears even in the face of unbearable losses. As a mother and as an artist, she has vowed to let her loved ones know they are valued and appreciated.

"Everyone needs the reassurance that they are loved," she stressed. "People need to hear it. In the end, that's all everyone is looking for, to know they are loved."

As if to underscore this uplifting message, she has created an explosion of colour in an idyllic meadow scene bursting with medicinal heart-shaped flowers. In the centre of *Flowers of Love*, a woman in blue gathers a bouquet of deep purple flowers to her breast. Behind her, a chorus of pale green trees, reminiscent of French artist, Monet, dance in the distance. Above her, the mauve sky vibrates with blue crescents. For the artist, the painting reiterates the knowledge that all plants have healing properties, all humans yearn for love.

"Our family always used to go to the forest, to the beach and to the family camp," she said. "I remember many stories told by my Dad and my uncles. A lot of my art is based on our traditions and our common practices in our cultural heritage."

As she continues to paint and to explore her memories, Mary has witnessed the mystical aspect of the process on more than once occasion. Works such as, *Healing Spirit of the Rattle* and *Other Side Beside Us*, have made her more conscious of the unseen forces at work when an artist puts brush to canvas. Sometimes the unexpected imagery can be unsettling.

"Sometimes you set out to do one scene, and something else emerges," she revealed. "Each painting truly has its own life force. At first this was frightening to me, but my brother helped me to share and to let other people see what's there."

Although there are many identifiable human and animal forms in many of her works, she has produced several abstract pieces as well. In *Water Spirits*, for example, conceptualized images of loons and fishes swirl through a sea of turquoise. And in *Connection*, the artist brings all the elements necessary for life together in an tribute to water, land and air.

Although Mary insists that she's still in the early developmental stages of her art, she has been enjoying some welcome recognition. She has participated in numerous juried exhibitions across Turtle Island including the Smithsonian Holiday Art Market in New York City, the Indigenous Peoples Art Competition in Mount Pleasant, Michigan and also has original work in the Art Guild Gallery in Toronto's Yorkville. She has also maintained a presence in the annual Manitoulin Art Tour with a display at the South Baymouth Gallery.

"It took me thirty years to circle around to my self and to see that I needed to paint and to find the confidence to do it. Sometimes we create our own barriers," she acknowledged.

Seeing a stage production dramatizing the life of Wikwemikong trailblazer, Daphne Odjig, had a profound effect on Mary as she worked to hone her own skills. De-ba-jeh-mu-jig Theatre Group had created a play based on the biography, history and legend paintings of the artist, known as the Queen of the Woodland School. Although she has finally found a home in the National Gallery of Canada, Daphne was a practising artist for decades before she received the accolades she merited. As a woman artist and a First Nations artist, she encountered widespread prejudice in the Canadian art establishment. For Mary, it was a moving experience to understand the obstacles that faced a woman pioneer artist from her home community.

Today, art continues to act as a catalyst for personal growth. Like Daphne Odjig, she rejoices at overcoming many of the stumbling blocks that held her back.

"Now today, I am able to receive my healing when I pick up the paintbrush and allow myself to fall into the world of colour," she said. "I love to play with acrylic paint, to make texture. I love seeing what comes into being. I never really know what is going to come to life on the canvas board when I sit down to paint a picture. It may be a memory picture, or it may be an abstract form. All I know is that my thoughts fly away, and I am gone from this world that I walk and breathe in, into a beautiful world of colour, one with no concept of time or problems, a swirling world of inner healing..."

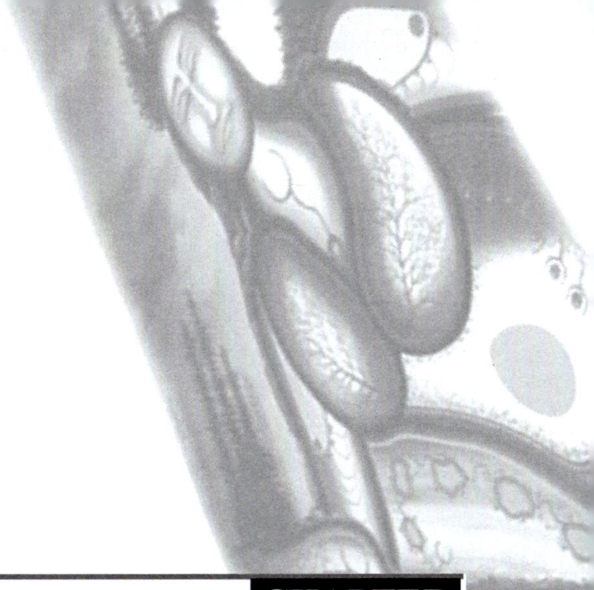

CHAPTER 14

JAMES SIMON MISHIBINIJIMA (1954 -): Master of Many Styles

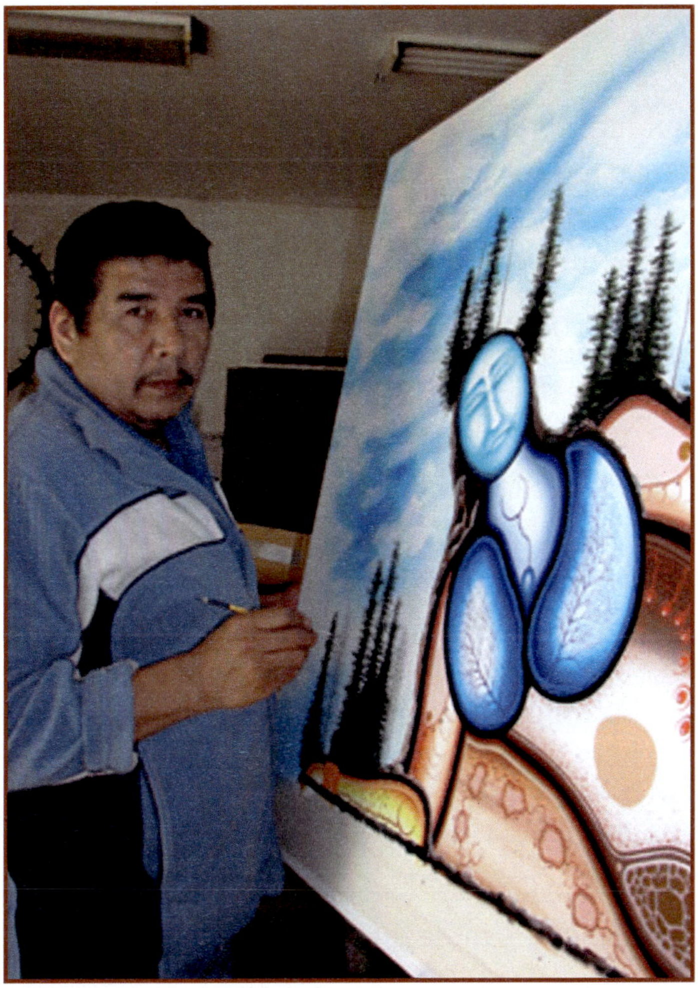

For the past four decades, Wikwemikong artist, Mishibinijima, has been exploring the islands and coves of Manitoulin, Birch Island and LaCloche, immersing himself in the spiritual energy of the land, water and sky. During these solitary excursions, he watches and listens until he senses it's time to capture the vision before him. From his visits to other scenic wonders such as Strawberry Island, Phillip Edward Island, Little Squaw Island, Flowerpot Island, Fisher Point, Cape Smith and Collin's Inlet, he has gathered inspiration for a series of paintings celebrating Mother Earth and her children.

He was born February 12, 1954 in Wikwemikong and was educated in North Bay and Manitoulin schools. When he was young, he was given the name, James Alexander

Simon by the missionaries who could not pronounce his name, but today he is known far and wide as Mishibinijima.

His paintings are exhibited in Canada and Europe as well as at American galleries in Michigan, Chicago, Indianapolis and Washington, DC.

Although he is an award winning painter, Mishibinijima did not foresee an artistic career when he was growing up on Manitoulin Island. In fact, he had set his sights on joining the RCMP when he finished high school. But sometimes forces beyond one's control can take over and a youth can find himself pulled in an unexpected direction.

"The art just made a path," he explained during a tour of his Lakeshore Road studio. "For instance, Francis Kagige, one of the pioneers of Wikwemikong (art), was my neighbour. And we used to go up to his little studio there and paint and he talked about his style. He also shared cultural teachings."

In those days, not too many families had television or radio, he noted, so story-telling was a natural diversion. Children had many opportunities to listen to legends and oral history shared by relatives and community elders.

Participation in an art club at Manitoulin Secondary School (circa 1969), also gave him a taste of what it might be like to earn his livelihood as an artist. Some of the young painters and carvers sold their works, thanks to the student art group, he reported.

In the years that followed, his community recognized his gifts and encouraged him to teach art in local schools. He also shared his artistic talents with classes as far afield as Sarnia and Lambton.

"I started to make a name for myself in the art world," he said. "I slowly built up some positive connections."

His career received a significant boost when he met a German fan of his paintings and he was invited to share his work with a larger European audience. In German centres such as Munster and Cologne, he was introduced to business executives who were very enthusiastic about collecting the works of Mishiminijima and passing the word on to their colleagues. His work caught on with the corporate clientele and from 1989 onward, he enjoyed the benefits of these influential contacts. By the fall of 2001 he was flying to Germany four or five times a year with selected paintings.

All of the attention was rewarding, and the growing demand for his work was gratifying for an artist, he acknowledged. Certainly, it was flattering to know that the astute people who collected European masters such as Monet and Picasso were also collecting Mishibinijima. But he soon realized that even his most ardent fans harboured misconceptions about the nature of art and about the unfolding of the creative process. In this fast-food, instant gratification world, a masterpiece cannot be created overnight. With sweatshops churning out mass-produced items in developing countries, it took a while for his customers to understand the patient and thoughtful approach involved in this heartfelt and meticulous art form. Eventually, his sponsors would learn to appreciate that a James Simon painting is labour intensive, to say the least.

Visitors will not see anything remotely resembling an assembly line production at his studio. In fact, it is not uncommon for him to work for three months on a single concept. Over the course of fifteen years, he might finish fifteen to twenty paintings of various styles. He estimates that he expresses himself in 18 different modes.

"I work constantly and I am never satisfied until that feeling comes to me that it is completed, or else I can't move on to the next painting," he revealed. "I'll work away at the minute details and then I will turn around and bury it."

Over the past forty years, Mishibinijima has certainly earned this freedom to refine and clarify his vision and his beliefs. Artificial deadlines would interfere with a process that is, of necessity, unhurried and contemplative. Because he expresses himself in several diverse techniques, he often feels compelled to abandon one project temporarily and attend to another. Shifting gears periodically helps to renew his spirit because there's a tremendous emotional, physical, mental and spiritual investment in a painting.

His *Mountain Series*, for example, has broad cross-cultural appeal and a strong following in North America and Europe. The dynamic canvases have won prizes at prestigious juried shows in Mount Pleasant, Indianapolis, Santa Fe and Connecticut. However, each work requires an intensity of focus and an attention to detail that are difficult to maintain for long stretches of time. He estimates that a single canvas may contain up to 32,000 shades of colour once it is near completion.

"The reason that I won first prize and best in show is that it totally overpowered all the other pieces," he said.

People who attend his shows or galleries frequently question him about his personal system of symbols. He's happy to respond to their interest and curiosity.

"It's just that everybody's intrigued," he acknowledged. "Why is this artist using diamonds in his paintings?," they ask. I explain to them that I use the diamonds in my work to express the sweat lodge stone for Mother Earth, the secret rock we call it."

For many years, countless observers have said to him, "You seem to see spirits in your paintings a lot. What does that spirit look like?" Every time they ask, he explains that it looks "like a diamond inside one person, just above his heart; that's where it just lights up. It's so perfect. And that's where we're entering once we leave the body, once the body has finished its functions. The circle doesn't end, it keeps on going. So that's why you see the diamond in each of the mountain pieces."

There are many examples of his ceremonial and respectful approach, but one of the most powerful, is a portrait he created for Pope John Paul II. Like many of his paintings, this monumental work is based on a vision he received in the summer of 2003. He recalls walking in the woods and being surrounded by cedar boughs. As he moved, he discovered a shimmering light and a small clearing in the forest. When he passed through the opening, he encountered the Pope. The Pontiff asked him, "Where is my rock, James?" Mishibinijima promised his ethereal visitor that he would make him the focus of his next painting.

Vatican officials were so enthralled with the completed image that they invited him to make a personal presentation to the Pope in October 2004. In the painting, Pope John Paul is shown in prayer with a full moon behind him reflecting off the island waters. Pictographs etched into his robes celebrate the spirit of peace and understanding that Pope brought during his travels in the Americas.

The meditative quality is also apparent in *Spirit Stream*, a painting based on a Wikwemikong legend he heard many times in his youth. According to this oft-told tale, portals to the spirit world exist all over Manitoulin Island. When people pray, the prayers enter into the "spirit holes" where they are answered.

"The spirits come through from the other side of the 'spirit holes' to have contact with the human world," he said. "There are spirits watching us and we are connected to the other side. Some day we will all be spirits going toward the light, trying to connect to the other side."

The ephemeral nature of the human passage through life is also emphasized in a work entitled, *Remembrance*. For Mishibinijima, every generation leaves behind a teaching for the generation to follow. As we live out our finite lives, those who have gone before us travel with us.

"Our journey takes a lifetime," he said."What's around us is always living, always looking at us. When we travel, the spirits are always with us; we are guarded by the spirits. They are walking with us."

The same painstaking work is evident in *The Child*, a painting inspired by Dreamer's Rock on the Whitefish River First Nation. As always, Mother Earth holds a place of honour in the landscape, watching over her children with maternal care and providing sustenance.

"The tree of life on the breasts is a sign of life," he said. "That's where we get our milk when we are children. We need her for us to survive; we need to live in balance with her. We need to hug the Earth."

An intimate and concentrated effort is required to commune with the spirits and to evoke these themes. Mountain pieces are so demanding that there's always the danger that the artist might "crash and burn." Fortunately, he knows his limits.

"I might spend three months on a mountain piece and then I'll be screaming for a pictograph or a book illustration," he confided. "And viewers are often surprised that I can shut off one energy and draw upon another. To them it's almost like it's a different artist at work. "Who is this person?," they might ask themselves, that he can switch from the mountain series, to pictographs, to watercolour illustrations. But I have mastered each style. It's all about energy; it's different types of energy. It's like a branch on a tree; maybe the mountain piece is the stem and all my other styles are each branch."

The mountain paintings have undoubtedly solidified his reputation both in Canada and abroad, however, his pictographs speak to many people as well. When he was younger, he had studied the ancient rock paintings in Minnesota and other sites, but his mentor, Sam Osawamick, had counselled him not to include them in his paintings. It was twenty-five years before the Wikwemikong Elder changed his mind and encouraged Mishibinijima to incorporate the old symbols into his contemporary work. One of his most compelling pieces is entitled, *The Water Keepers*. It depicts four towering figures, reminiscent of stilt walkers, peering into their reflection in a pond. As they gaze down upon us, we can feel the caring in their demeanor. The sky behind them blazes with brilliant yellow and red. The images represent the four nations responsible for guarding over the Great Lakes, the Ojibwe, Odawa, Potawatomi and Menomonee.

Throughout his *Speaking Pictographs Project*, Mishibinijima has emphasized the importance of the Great Lakes watershed to all life on Turtle Island. As he has written, "The North American people need to take notice that the people from this continent are living on a very destructive path. And the path they are leaving behind for future generations is just illness for animal, land and the human body."

Through an online blog and his powerful artwork, the artist has repeatedly urged his fellow human beings to take care of the freshwater lakes. "Destroy the water and we destroy ourselves," he reminded visitors to his website.

Similar life-affirming messages have been articulated in the Shki-Mawtch Taw-win En-mook curriculum materials he created for Kenjgewin Teg Educational Institute (KTEI) on M'Chigeeng First Nation. In lavishly illustrated books such as *The Loon's Necklace* and *Shiime*, he has reiterated the necessity of learning survival skills and striving to be one with our natural surroundings. Other titles, including, *The Creation of Turtle Island* and *Mdaamin* also emphasized the importance of balanced living and protecting the gifts of Creation.

For Mishibinijima, the role of teacher and artist are often intertwined. As an educator, he shares the humanitarian teachings he learned while he was growing up. "As adults we have to guide the children into the future," he said. "We are the teachers. It is important that the illustrations nourish the child. For children we have to come to a place where a child can grow."

So in preparing the materials aimed at a younger audience he has chosen a gentle approach to avoid overwhelming receptive young minds. Some of his other modes of expression often assail the viewer with a firestorm of colour and imagery. For some, the barrage can be very cathartic and emotional, perhaps even unsettling. In his view, the water colour effect he has adapted brings the youngsters into the teachings in a soothing, non-threatening fashion.

"It allows the child to grow into colour, to grow into the theme, to grow into the surroundings. The calmness of the water colour effect doesn't just happen," he stressed. "It comes slowly like a birth, like the rebirth of a thought, of a theme. On the other hand, if I used a mountain piece as an illustration, it would totally bombard their way of thinking; it would be too much to have everything coming at them like lightning."

Consequently, the humans in his stories are often depicted in serene settings, perhaps sitting under a maple tree or on a rock or beside the water. The reader senses that they are one with the Earth, that they are offered everything they need in the way of resources and medicine. And when humans are shown engaged in ceremonies, a soft green light bathes them in protection and empathy. When humans mourn, the birds, animals and spirits mourn too. But when humans awake to their own potential and strength, the sky erupts in roman candles throwing meteor showers of joy and communion.

In his book illustrations, the universe seems to vibrate with positive energy as it pulsates with hypnotic blues, purples and greens. There's always a tremulous, dancing light behind the plants such as corn and raspberries. And instinctively all living things lean towards the light.

His story *Shkimma and Sam* underscores the importance of having mentors to guide children on "the good path." In one section, the reader observes Shkimma's spirit curled up inside him in the fetal position. He hasn't given himself a chance to grow and develop. However, the child is fortunate to meet Sam, an elder who is able to touch the child and awaken his spirit. Sam uses gentle teasing and wise words to establish rapport with Shkimma.

Mishibinijima has enjoyed his association with Kenjgewin Teg. In addition to illustrating culturally appropriate teaching materials, he has supported the institute in raising funds for a new classroom facility. The $2.8 million capital building campaign was launched to help the school move out of its cramped quarters and into a modern facility designed to offer training and professional development programs for eight member First Nations. Corporate sponsors of the initiative were presented with framed prints of his work, entitled, *New Pathways*.

The gift is appropriate on many levels as it symbolizes both the new direction taken by Kenjgewin Teg and the new pathways opening up for First Nations students. And, of course, it reminds the community that James Simon has opened up new fields of vision for us and altered our perspectives on the world through his art and his philosophy.

Mishibinijima continues to prod the conscience of modern man and to promote the ideals of peace and balanced living. In the process, he draws his inspiration from diverse sources. For instance, in the summer of 2007, a vision of the late John F. Kennedy moved him to create another memorable canvas calling for global unity. In the dream, the late President of the United States echoed his famous inaugural speech: "Ask not what your country can do for you; ask what you can do for your country."

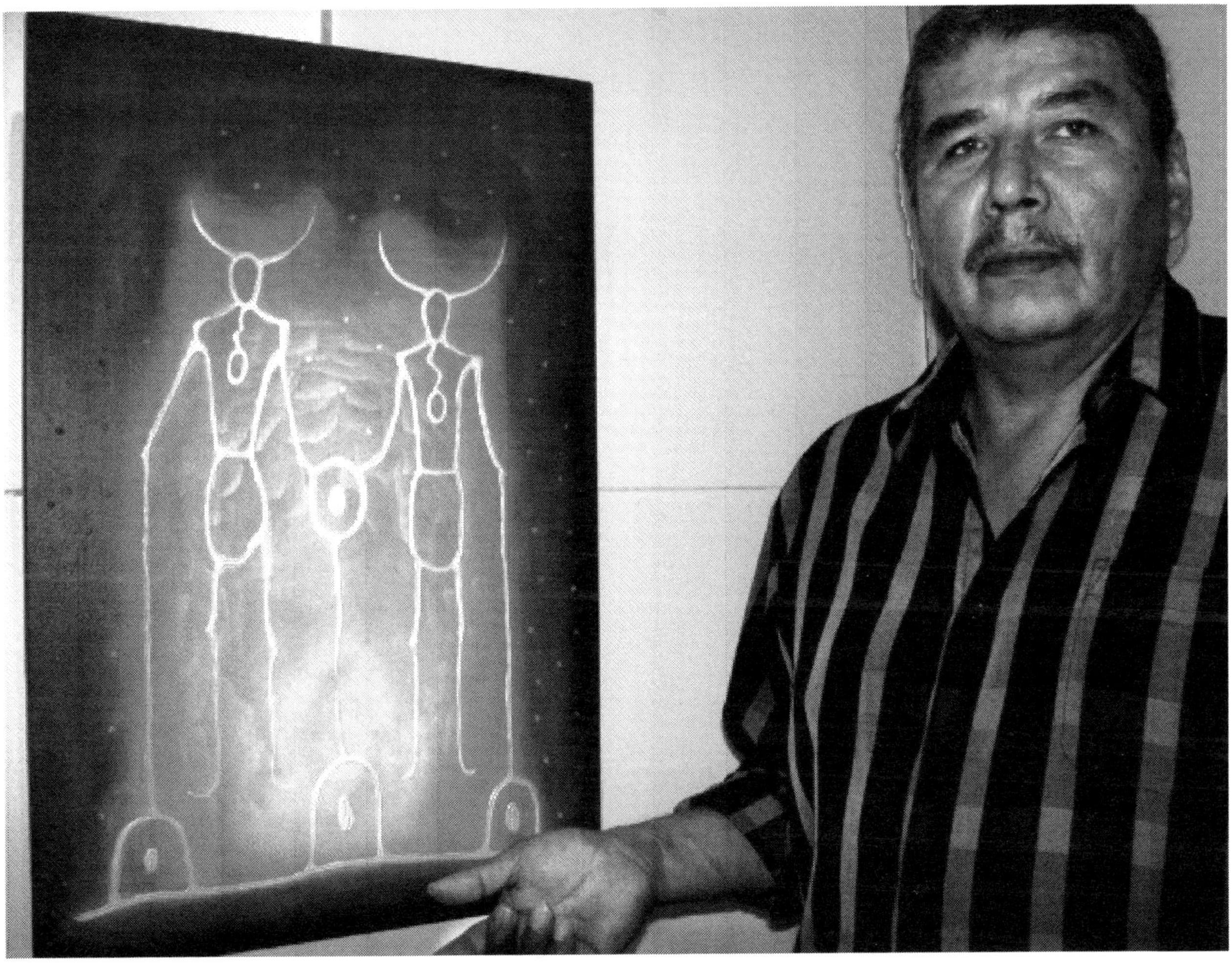

In the painting, Mishibinijima depicts the figure of JFK rising up on the right hand side of the canvas surrounded by bluish, purple light. At the President's side is an Eagle staff inlaid with a dream catcher and colourful ribbons dancing in the wind.

"A staff throughout time has represented dialogue in Native American culture," he said. "I placed a dream catcher holding four sacred eagle feathers honouring the four directions on Mother Earth which are white, yellow, red and black. These four colours of Mother Earth need to stand together in brotherhood for humanity. They need to share the cultures for greater understanding."

As his message circles out across the globe, it is certain that this master of many styles will continue to touch people's hearts through his art. He will continue to teach by example and to challenge others to do their part to foster peace and dialogue.

Because he has listened to the voices of the land, he has been able to shape his images and his themes carefully and precisely. Today his paintings have an enduring, timeless quality. As a member of the bear clan, he understands his responsibility to guard the medicines, protect the people and preserve the stories. For him it is important to share his beliefs, the lessons from life's journey and to pass them on before it is his turn to connect to the spirit world. It's a legacy to be proud of. Undoubtedly, his uplifting messages will reverberate through Time.

As Mishibinijima says,"We pass on what we know to all people in what we leave behind."

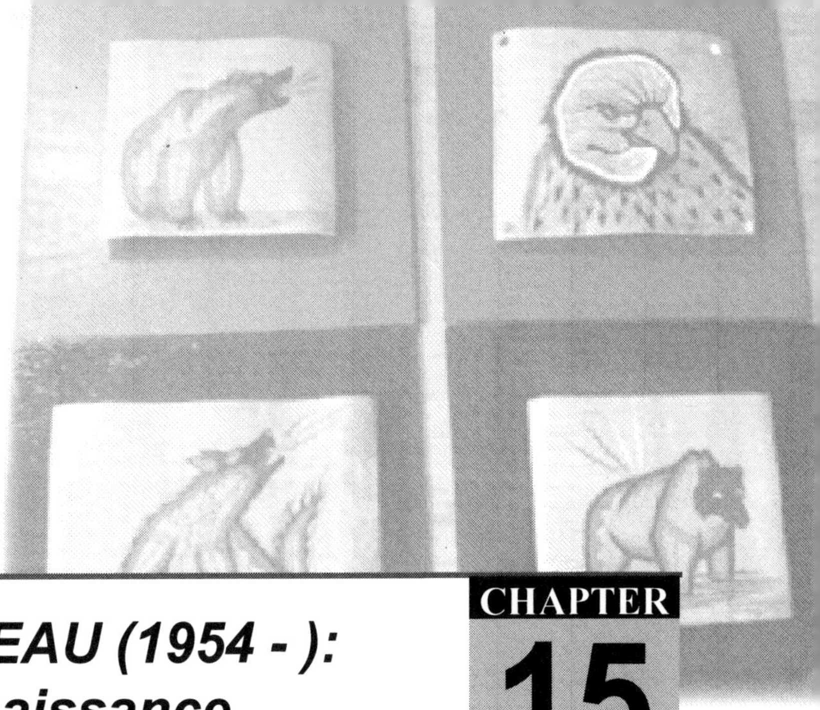

RANDY C. TRUDEAU (1954 -): Spiritual Renaissance

CHAPTER 15

In his youth, Randy C. Trudeau had established a solid reputation in the art world with exhibitions in Toronto, Vancouver, Halifax, Edmonton and the Yukon. *Anishnabe Mee-Kun*, a catalogue issued by the Ojibwe Cultural Foundation in 1984, described his work as a "lyrical artistic style distinguished by tonal form lines in four parallel bands of colour and his own unique method of depicting spiritual beings."

Beth Southcott, author of *The Sound of the Drum*, was equally complimentary in her 1985 overview of the Manitoulin School of Art. She praised him for inventing his own method of depicting invisible forces and noted that his mighty fists had produced many delicate brush strokes.

Born in 1954, Randy grew up in Buzwah on the shores of Manitowaning Bay and absorbed a wealth of cultural teachings from his grandfather. He enjoyed watching his grandfather whittle toy canoes as he shared entertaining and instructive stories with the children around him. At age seventeen, Randy was further influenced by the *Tales of Nokomis*, a book by Patronella Johnston, illustrated by Wikwemikong's pioneer painter, Francis Kagige. While attending Manitoulin Secondary School, Randy was a mainstay in the Indian Art Club and produced many works featuring his favourite subjects, including the bear, otter and eagle. Other than the high school classes and a summer arts program at Laurentian University, he received no formal training. He has developed accuracy and originality by studying his subjects closely and expressing his love of Creation on canvas, birchbark and drum.

After graduation, the Ojibwe Cultural Foundation invited Randy to share his techniques and reverence for the environment with youngsters in his community. He went on to teach art for four years in three Wikwemikong schools. In addition, he worked with friend and colleague, James Simon, to decorate the Wikwemikong Recreation and Cultural Centre with thunderbird and bear motifs.

From 1974 until 1982, he exhibited widely and his works were purchased by the McMichael gallery, the Royal Ontario Museum and the Ojibwe Cultural Foundation. Private collectors were also enthusiastic about his unique works.

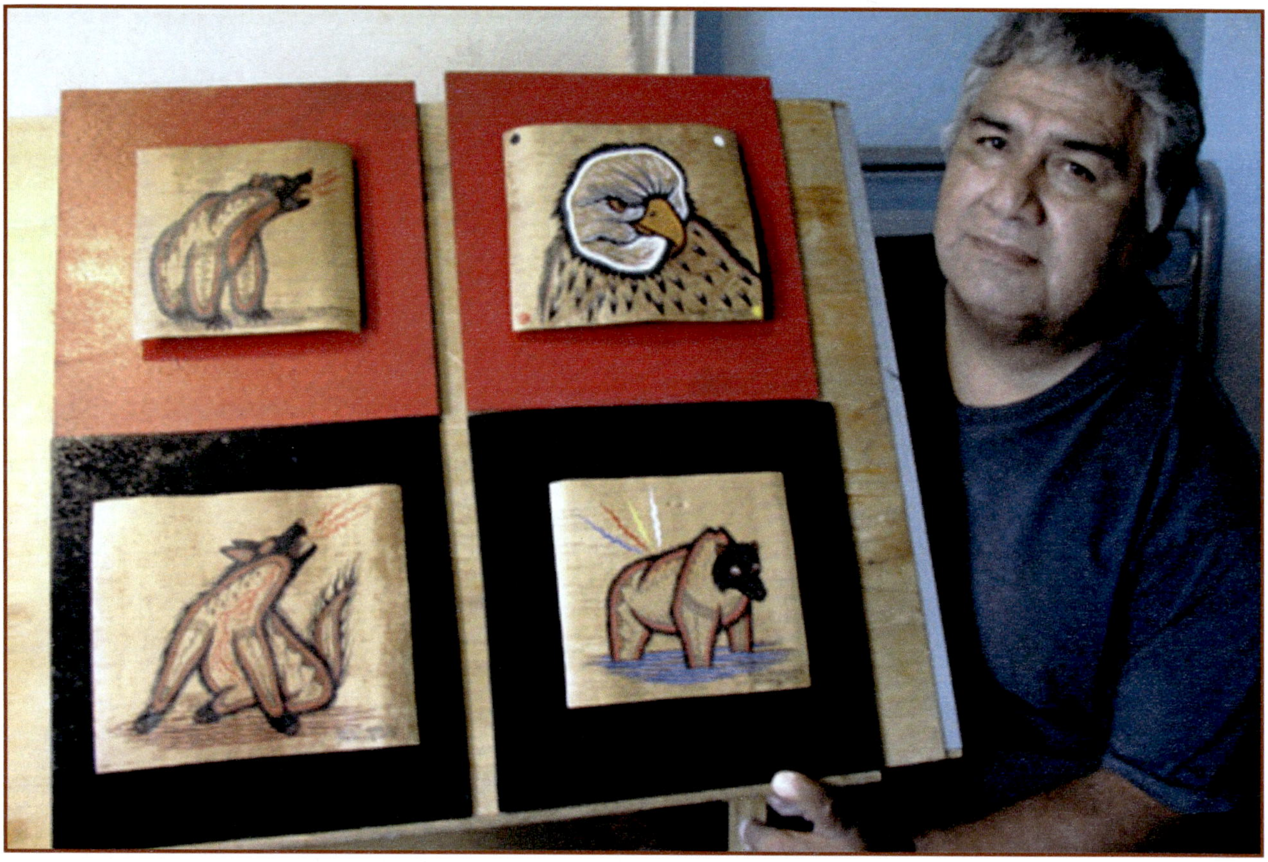

Randy had embarked upon his art career at a time when First Nations artists were enjoying a period of relatively strong public support and adulation during the 1970s and the 1980s; however, economic recession and changing tastes led to hardship and disinterest during the 1990s and into the new millennium.

"I stopped painting because the art world was going down and I found I had to underprice myself," Randy said during a tour of his home studio. "I painted until the 90s and then I experienced a little dry spell. The art business was struggling, so I took time off to take a heavy equipment course and to become self-employed. My priority then was to feed my family."

As he ran his own business and attended to the practicalities of making a livelihood, the art remained on the back burner. It would take a personal health crisis to bring him back full circle to his first calling.

At age fifty, Randy was enjoying a hockey game on television when he suddenly collapsed and fell to the floor. He was hospitalized for weeks in Sudbury as doctors tried to prevent his kidneys from shutting down.

During this traumatic period, he experienced an out of body experience that would forever alter his perspective and set him on a new path.

"I saw myself walking on air somewhere over Science North," he said. "I saw beautiful land and forests and then I saw someone beckon to me. I followed a narrow trail through the forest. In the vision, people were dressed just the way they used to look a long time ago. The ladies had kerchiefs on their heads; all the traditionally dressed people were there with all the modern dressed ones too. All the people from the past and present were all together. And there were lots of birds and animals. It was so beautiful."

Although the dreamscape was soothing and alluring, Randy was frightened and chose not to remain with the people of his vision. "I looked around and I couldn't see my shadow," he recalled. "I got scared and I came back home. It wasn't time for me to go."

In the aftermath of his near death experience, Randy struggled to regain his health and to make major lifestyle changes. During his recuperation, concerned family members urged him to start painting again. By March of 2008 he was revisiting the imagery and the stories that had inspired him in his youth.

He speaks fondly of his childhood and the opportunity he had for a close relationship with his grandparents, Ignatius and Mary Olive Trudeau. His grandfather was a skilled carver and his grandmother created sweetgrass and birchbark crafts. Both taught Randy the importance of respecting animals and making use of every part of the animal including hide, bones, meat and claws.

In the 1950s and 1960s, many Manitoulin families survived by keeping extensive gardens and eating wild game meat. Some First Nations artisans also made handicrafts for the island's tourist trade in Little Current. Randy's imagination was ignited at a young age as he witnessed his grandfather outwit and harvest a wily porcupine.

As an adult he speaks affectionately of his mentors. "My grandfather would tell us stories after supper; that's how I learned," he said. "And I also heard stories from Francis Kagige. I was able to visualize the characters in the stories."

Randy also remains nostalgic about time spent at the Schreiber Island summer art camps operated by the Manitou Arts Foundation, during the 1970s. "We had a lot of fun," he said. "Most of us were just eighteen and we had a chance to learn our history and do sketches. Some awesome pictures came out of that time. We all learned from each other; that's the best thing of all."

He also enjoyed participating in the Ojibwe Cultural Foundation art camps. And he still expresses admiration for mentors such as Daphne Odjig, Carl Beam, Roy Thomas, Norval Morrisseau and Francis Kagige.

The spiritual practices, reinforced during the summer art camps, left a lasting impression on Randy and he continues to express gratitude to the Creator for the gifts in his life.

With the encouragement of his family, Randy renewed his commitment to the art in 2008. Once he started doing sketches again, he found the images coming fast and furious. All of the ideas stored up over the past few years came pouring out on to canvas and birchbark.

"It feels good to pick up the brushes again," he said. "It felt strange at first. I was worried because I was shaking, but once I started painting again the shakiness went away and the pictures flowed from heart to mind to canvas. Something was telling me that it was time to paint again."

The renaissance of Randy C. Trudeau was evident in an exhibition entitled, "The Teachings," mounted at the Gore Bay Museum and Heritage Centre in 2008. As they had been in the past, viewers were struck by his sensitive depictions of birds, animals and humans.

"The animals try to tell people how important they are," he said. "The paintings tell the purpose of the animals and explain their relationship to people. Also every bird has a purpose; there is a reason why they are here on Earth; they have things to teach us."

In his view, humans can learn valuable lessons from the tenacity of the beaver, the swiftness of the otter, the strength of the bear, the diligence of the hummingbird and the generosity of the loon.

In a recent flurry of creativity, Randy drew upon many different Ojibwe, Odawa and Cree influences as he resumed the passionate preoccupation of his youth. He has also been inspired to carve Moose antlers and bone.

"Now that I've started painting again, the work is entirely different from those I used to do," he said. "In the past I did realistic pictures of animals. Bears, eagles and wolves were my specialty. But back then people often interpreted my portraits of animals as mean and vicious. In the new work I often paint dreams and visions. Spirituality is very much present in the new material. People have noticed that my painting has changed; they feel the warmth and the harmony that comes through."

Today Randy uses his artwork to raise funds for the Kidney Foundation and his work is again visible in Manitoulin galleries and shops.

Although there was a brief gap in the continuity of his work, Randy has emerged from the hiatus with a deepened understanding of himself, his heritage and his art. Sometimes a period of inactivity can be misinterpreted as a dry spell, when in actuality, it may signal the beginning of a dynamic new phase of artistic life.

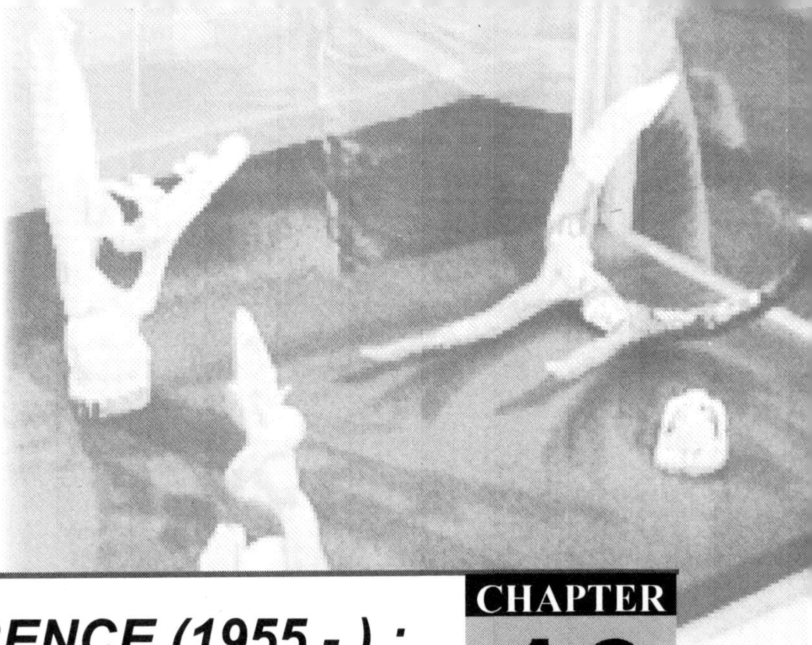

GORDON WAINDUBENCE (1955 -) : Giving His Gifts Away

CHAPTER 16

Although his eyesight no longer allows him to produce his extraordinary works of art, Gordon Waindubence of Sheguiandah First Nation will long be revered as a master self-taught carver. During a highly productive period in the 1980s, he fashioned over four hundred finely detailed pieces, many destined to become collector's treasures.

Today, his intricate wood, ivory and stone creations are on display at the Museum of Civilization in Hull, Quebec, the Royal Ontario Museum in Toronto, Lillian's Museum in M'Chigeeng and in numerous private collections in Canada, the United States and overseas.

Like many artists, Gordon faced daunting hurdles in his youth and experienced some serious setbacks. And like many other creative individuals, he eventually discovered that art was a vehicle for self-examination and personal growth. He freely shares the struggles he went through as a young man searching for meaning and a sense of purpose.

"In the 1970s, I worked in the mines in Sudbury for eight years or so," he said during a viewing of his work at the Ojibwe Cultural Foundation. "At that time I was in a different lifestyle; you wouldn't have wanted to know me back then. You needed alcohol to work in the dark, wet mines."

However, two significant life events would serve as a wake-up call and lead him to sobriety. The birth of his youngest son inspired him to make some positive changes. Also, a catastrophic mine accident left him shaken and searching for answers.

By 1978, he had left his work in the mines and embarked on a phase of intensive soul-searching. For a period he worked at whatever job happened to be available.

At first, he sought guidance from friends and during the next few years, he would find spiritual helpers in the prairie provinces as well as the Dakotas. He listened to the stories and the legends; he immersed himself in the ceremonies and he received much understanding along the way.

"I had no identity at that time," he confided. "I didn't know who I was. In fact, I was just roaming around and I didn't know what I was looking for. It is really hard to find yourself."

During his spiritual quest, he was introduced to carving by one of his mentors in 1978. Over the course of several days he watched and listened as the Elder shared his knowledge. Although it was not readily apparent to Gordon at the time, he would soon perceive that a new path was opening up for him.

"I came to realize that the most valuable gifts come from the heart," he said. "The man had promised to give me a gift that no one could ever take away from me."

Fortunately for the art world, Gordon accepted his affinity for fine sculpture and never ceased to be grateful for the promise.

Gradually, he began to get his bearings and to this day he often meditates on the teachings shared with him during those troubled times. For him, it is very important to listen to as many different mentors as possible in order to learn balance.

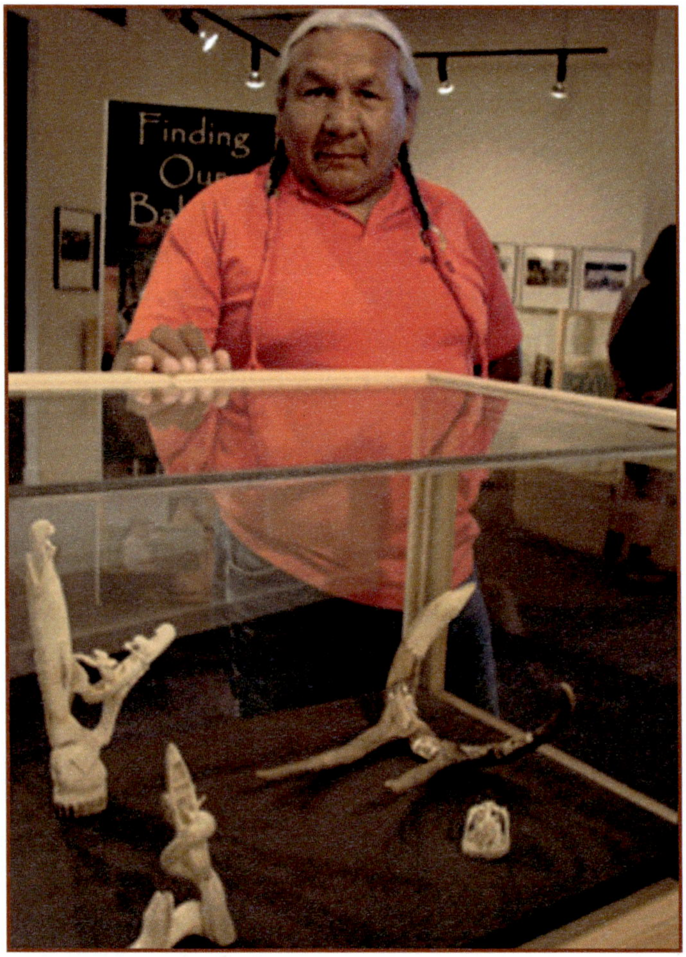

"I had six different mentors over the years and they have all passed on," he said. "But I can still hear them."

Woodworking seemed to speak to him early on. Another Grandfather engaged his help to cut truck loads of wood to take to a sweat lodge. In the process of harvesting trees, Gordon learned to use timbering equipment such as chain saws, knives and axes. His friend showed him how to visualize images with the natural shapes and shades in trees and how to fashion a rudimentary totem pole.

"The first one I made was pretty darn rough," he laughed."I wanted to take it home, but I couldn't. So I gave it away."

He remembers experimenting with carving in the early 80s and giving away the first pieces he made to family members.

His philosophy hasn't changed much over the decades. He still believes in giving it away, his gift, his knowledge, his hope, "to anyone who wants to listen." He has volunteered time in many organizations, offering his listeners guidance to a new lifestyle and introducing them to the stories, songs, beliefs, customs and ceremonies of Anishinaabe culture. He often counsels youth who are in conflict with the law and tries to steer them to the Red Path.

"We have to give humankind opportunities," he said. "If we don't, they take the long way around. As one of my mentors told me, the Red Road you seek runs between the mind and the heart. It's a very short distance, but it might take you a lifetime to see where you belong in the circle of life."

His first carvings may have been "rough," in his estimation, but over the years he honed his skills in both wood, ivory and stone. Before long, he had gained a reputation as a remarkably accomplished self-taught artist. Many people were drawn to admire and to collect his exquisitely polished and refined artworks.

As an art practice, carving is very demanding: physically, mentally, emotionally and spiritually. To achieve the fine detail that characterizes his work, one needs excellent eyesight, a steady hand, patience and extreme flexibility.

"Stone and ivory carvings are very unforgiving," Gordon stressed. "One mistake and you have to be ready to initiate Plan B."

Viewers still marvel at the finesse required to sculpture everything from intricate flowers and fish scales to tiny dancers and warriors. How did he possibly carve the miniature teeth in the narrow mouths or the realistic ribs in the bear figures? To say the work is labour intensive, is an under statement.

"When you work with ivory and bone, you have to get past the smell," he said. "You have to have proper ventilation and proper lighting. And then you have to cross your fingers (and toes, and eyes) to ensure that it doesn't get broken."

Mishaps are bound to occur, despite all the precautions an artist takes; however, gluing is never an option.

Most of his artworks are very fragile and need to be handled with utmost care. Only by holding them up and turning them, can the viewer fully appreciate the extent of the detail and precision. Every piece is original right down to the specks of dried blood embedded on the antler or the bone. Because they are one of a kind, duplicates cannot be made.

To cope with the demands of carving, he often worked on several pieces simultaneously. For instance, he would shape a fish and then set it aside for a while and go on to chisel a serpent or a turtle image elsewhere.

As with all great art, there is an element of magic involved in the process. Sometimes, if he set a project aside for a few weeks, he might find a new image calling to him upon his return. He was always surprised when people wanted to buy the carvings even before they were finished.

Undoubtedly, people are attracted to his work because it is completely original and in harmony with nature.

"I always aim to leave things the way they are and retain the natural shades," he said. "I don't use shellac because that turns yellow. And I don't use preservatives, just elbow grease."

In addition to being an exquisite craftsman, Gordon is also an inventor. He has been forced to modify, or make his own tools, in order to achieve the detailed work in his sculptures. Like his carvings, Gordon Waindubence remains one of a kind.

He has set aside his tools, but he has never set aside his desire to help others. Since 1995 he has served as the regional Elder for the Union of Ontario Indians. He has also assisted his home community with the building of a roundhouse in Sheguiandah First Nation in 2003.

In 2005 he was part of a very significant event. He led a ceremony during which two nations, the Metis Nation and the Anishinabek Nations, came together as one, in an historic gathering to smoke the Pipe of Peace, something that hadn't happened in two hundred years. As an Anishinabek Nation Elder, Gordon serves 42 communities in the Lake Huron Region, the South West Region, the South East Region and Lake Superior Region.

In 2009 he continued to share his knowledge with a whole new generation of First Nations youth during Youth and Elders gatherings hosted by the Ojibwe Cultural Foundation in M'Chigeeng.

• • • •

References

Arrowsmith, Lisa. "Canadian Doctor Hits the Road: Aboriginal physician travels world to study shamans, healers for new series." Sudbury Star 17 Aug. 2007: B6.

Art Gallery of Ontario. www.ago.net

Bradley, Lara. "Finally Odjig's Work Recognized: Sudbury Exhibit Just the First Stop for a Brilliant but Often overlooked Artist." Sudbury Star 20 Sept. 2007: C1.

Bradley, Lara. "Odjig Retrospective a Coup for Art Gallery." Sudbury Star 27, Dec. 2007: C1.

Canada Council for the Arts. www.canadacouncil.ca

Canada Council Art Bank. "Carl Beam RCA (1943-2005)." Monthly Bulletin 15 Sept. 2005: www.artbacnk.ca

CBC Arts. "Ojibwa Artist Carl Beam Dies." 9 Aug. 2005: www.cbc.ca

Canadian Press. "The Real Morrisseau." Sudbury Star 26 Mar. 2005: C1 Canadian Press. "Morrisseau Dead at 75." Sudbury Star 6 Dec. 2007

Centre for Contemporary Canadian Art, Canadian Art Database, Faculty of Fine Arts, York University. www.ccca.ca

Cinader, Bernhard."Manitoulin Island - The Third Layer." Curator's Statement. Thunder Bay, Ontario: 3 April to 24 May, 1987.

Corbiere, Alan. "An Ode to Woodpeckers: The Woodland School of Art." Ojibwe Cultural Foundation Newsletter: July 2008, Vol 3, Issue 3: 2.

Cybermuse Artist's Page. Your Art Education Research Site. www.cybermuse.gallery.ca

Devine, Bonnie. Daphne Odjig: A Retrospective Exhibition. Ottawa: National Gallery of Canada, 2007.

Dobrovnik, Frank. "Survivor Still Waiting for Apology." Sudbury Star 4 May 2007: A5.

Eichorn, Virginia MacDonnell. "It's All Relative." Curator's Statement. 9 Oct. 2004: Canadian Clay and Glass Gallery.

Gessel, Paul. "Flying Still: Carl Beam 1943-2005." Ottawa Citizen 8 Dec. 2005.

Grande, John K. "Carl Beam: Dissolving Time." Balance: Art and Nature. Black Rose Books: Montreal, 1994.

Henry, Victoria. Canada Council Art Bank. Curator's Statement. www.carelton.ca

Hill, Greg A. Norval Morrisseau: Shaman Artist. Ottawa: National Gallery of Canada, 2006.

Keeptwo, Suzanne. "Odjig Exhibit a Statement of Identity." Ontario Birchbark April 2008: 21.

Kelly, Lindsay. "The Artist as Social Critic: Blake Debassige Speaks About Fairness to Artists, political honesty and more." Manitoulin Expositor 12 Sept. 2007: A1.

Kelly, Lindsay. "M'Chigeeng First Nation Artist Presents First-hand Insight into Thirty Year Career." Manitoulin Expositor 12 Sept. 2007: A17.

Kelly, Lindsay. "From Pain Emerges Beauty in the Work of Mary Pheasant." Manitoulin Expositor 11 June 2008: 17.

Kivinen-Newman, Chris. "Fledgling Weengushk film Institute given $35,000 Grant by CTV Network." Manitoulin Expositor 24 Sept. 2008: 13.

Little, Margo. "Take Time to Listen to the Holy Buzz." Highgrader Spring 2007: 11-13.

Little, Margo. "Artist Publishes Story for Children of all Ages." Highgrader Spring 2007: 9-11

Little, Margo. "Portrait of the Artist as Dragon Slayer." Highgrader Summer 2007: 31-33.

Little, Margo. "Manitoulin Potter's Ceramic Messages." Highgrader Late Summer 2007: 18-19.

Little, Margo. "Spider Island Revisited: Leland Bell Reflects on Schreiber Island Art Camp." Highgrader Fall 2007: 11-13.

Little, Margo. "Shirley Cheechoo: A Long Legacy of Storytelling." Highgrader Winter 2008:14-16

Little, Margo. "Morrisseau: Mentor to Many Generations of Native Artists." Highgrader Spring 2008: 27-29.

Little, Margo. "Creating New Pathways: The Art of Mishibinijima." Highgrader Summer 2008: 9-11.

Little, Margo. "Burying the Ruler: Carl Beam (1943-2005)." Highgrader Summer 2008: 11-13.

Little, Margo. "Exploring Memory with Maaniinhs." Highgrader Late Summer 2008: 18-20.

Little, Margo. "Melvin Madahbee: Coming Full Circle." Highgrader Late Summer 2008: 21-22.

Little, Margo. "Gordon Waindubence: Sheguiandah's Master Carver." Highgrader Autumn 2008: 33-35.

Little, Margo. "Don Ense: Drawing Upon Memories for Inspiration." Highgrader Christmas 2008: 18-21.

Little, Margo. "Francis Peter Kagige: Pioneer Woodland Artist Served as Mentor to Many." Highgrader Winter 2009: 19-21.

Little, Margo. "A Posthumous Tribute to Martin Panamick." Highgrader Spring 2009: 17-19.

Little, Margo. "Manitoulin Model Takes New York by Storm: Shirley Cheechoo makes Successful Excursion." Manitoulin Recorder 1 May 1985: Vol 74.

Little, Margo. "Island Film Maker Heads to Toronto: Shirley Cheechoo Accepted into Canadian Film Centre." Ontario Birchbark May 2002: 3.

Little, Margo. "Manitoulin Art Tour Showcases Island Creativity." Ontario Birchbark July 2002: 10.

Little, Margo. "Weengushk Film Institute Nurturing First Nations Screenwriters." Ontario Birchbark February 2009:Vol 26, #11.

Little, Margo. "Top Artist to Return to Manitoulin." Sudbury Star 18 June 2004: A2.

Little, Margo. "Artist's Impact Felt from Island to Ottawa." Sudbury Star 29 Mar. 2005: A2.

Little, Margo. "Daphne Odjig Retrospective Exhibition Long Overdue, Curator Says." Manitoulin Expositor 12 Sept. 2007: 16.

Little, Margo. "Opening Ceremonies Held for Daphne Odjig Retrospective." Manitoulin Expositor 19 Sept. 2007: 17.

Little, Margo. "Crucible of Creativity: The Manitou Arts Flourish." Witness: A Symposium on the Woodland School. Sudbury, Ontario: Laurentian University, October 11-14, 2007.

Little, Margo. "Art Retrospective a Major Triumph for Wikwemikong's Daphne Odjig." Manitoulin Expositor 17 Oct. 2007: A1.

Little, Margo. "Manitoulin Well-represented at Woodland School Conference." Manitoulin Expositor 24 Oct. 2007: 1A.

Little, Margo. "Leland Bell Shares his Artistic Vision with OCF Audience." Manitoulin Expositor 24 Oct. 2007: 5A.

Little, Margo. "David Migwans Offers Pottery Workshops." Manitoulin Expositor 7 May 2008: 9.

Little, Margo. "Outdoor Firing Kiln Provides Unique Experience for Pottery Students." Manitoulin Expositor 23 July 2008: 7A.

Little, Margo. "Planetary Concerns Inform New Ann Beam Work on Display in Gore Bay." Manitoulin Expositor 17, Sept. 2008: 6A.

Little, Margo. "Wikwemikong Artist Experiences Renaissance in 2008." Manitoulin Expositor 1 Oct. 2008: 5A.

Little, Margo. "Anishinabe Youth and Elders Come Together." Manitoulin Expositor 4 Feb. 2009: 1A.

Little, Margo. "A Posthumous Tribute to Martin Panamick" Highgrader Spring 2009: 17-19.

McCutcheon, Alicia: "Manitoulin Mosaic Highlights Wasse-Abin Student Talent." Manitoulin Expositor 11 June 2008:1A.

Meili, Dianne. "Physician Travels the World to Meet Healers." Windspeaker October 2007: 16.

Moodie, Jim. "Squaw Islands Renamed After Key Wiky Women." Manitoulin Expositor 15 Aug. 2007: A1.

Moodie, Jim. "Shirley Cheechoo, Dave Nahwegahbow Win National Acclaim." Manitoulin Expositor 21 Nov. 2007: 14.

Moodie, Jim. "Island Home to Three National Honorees." Manitoulin Expositor 12 Mar. 2008: A1.

Mulligan, Carol. "Healing Takes MD Around World." Sudbury Star 4 Sept. 2007: A1.

National Association of Indian Friendship Centres. "Native Fine Arts in Canada." The Native Perspective, Vol 3, Number 2, 1978: 47.

National Gallery of Canada. www.national.gallery

Neon Raven Gallery. www.neonravenartgallery.com

Ojibwe Cultural Foundation. K'wech-Ku-da-d'win: Native Provincial Craft Conference Report. Mississauga, Ontario: 3 June, 1981.

Ojibwe Cultural Foundation. Master Plan Study: Study for a new Ojibwe Cultural Centre. M'Chigeeng: Draft final report, July 1995.

Ojibwe Cultural Foundation. "The Unexplained." OCF Newsletter. Vol. 1, Issue 4, Oct. 2006.

Ontario Historical Society. "OCF Kicks off Construction of New Home." OHS Bulletin Toronto: September/October 1997.

Ontario Historical Society. "Mary Lou Fox Radulovich Passes Away." Toronto: July 1998.

Royal Ontario Museum Ethnology Department. Contemporary Native Art of Canada Manitoulin Island. Toronto: 11 July to 30 Sept., 1978.

Ryan, Allan J. "Carl Beam." The Trickster Shift: Humour and Irony in Contemporary Native Art. Vancouver and Seattle: UBC Press and University of Washington Press, 1999.

Sibbald, Barbara. "The Artist's Journey." CMA Media Inc.

Smith, Theresa S. The Island of the Anishnaabeg: Thunderers and Water Monsters In the Traditional Ojibwe Life-World. Idaho: University of Idaho Press, 1995.

Southcott, Mary E. The Sound of the Drum: The Sacred Art of the Anishnabec. Erin, Ontario: Boston Mills Press, 1985.

Vanderburgh, R.M. and M.E. Southcott. A Paintbrush in my Hand: Daphne Odjig Toronto: Natural Heritage/Natural History Inc., 1992.

Vervoort, Patricia. "A Visual Autobiography: Self-portraits of Carl Beam." First Nations, First Thoughts Conference. University of Edinburgh: 5 May, 2005. www.cst.ed.ac.uk

Wall, Petra: "Francis Peter Kagige: Now and Then." Manitoulin Expositor 31, Oct. 2007: 5.

Watson, Scott. "Land, Spirit, Power: First Nations at the National Gallery of Canada." Canadian Art Spring 1993, Vol 10, Number 1: 34.

Williams, Garett. "Celebrating Anishinaabe Art: For Three Weeks the Manitou Collection Will be at Fielding Park." Sudbury Star 10 May 2007: C1.

Zacharjewicz, Neil. "Mary Lou Fox Honoured at OCF." Manitoulin Recorder 8 Oct. 1997.

• • • •

Ordering Information

To order Portraits of Spirit Island: The Manitoulin School of Art Comes of Age, send cheque or money order to Box 79, Gore Bay ON P0P 1H0 or call 705-282-1714 or fax 705-282-1717. More information available at www.margolittle.com.